PENGUIN BOOKS
AI WEIWEI SPEAKS

Ai Weiwei is a Chinese artist, designer, architect, curator, poet, blogger and publisher.

Hans Ulrich Obrist is a curator and writer. Since 2006 he has been Co-director of the Serpentine Gallery, London.

Ai Weiwei Speaks

WITH

HANS ULRICH OBRIST

PENGUIN BOOKS

PENGUIN BOOKS

Published by the Penguin Group
Penguin Books Ltd, 80 Strand, London WC2R ORL, England
Penguin Group (USA) Inc., 375 Hudson Street, New York, New York 10014, USA
Penguin Group (Canada), 90 Eglinton Avenue East, Suite 700, Toronto, Ontario, Canada M4P 2Y3
(a division of Pearson Penguin Canada Inc.)
Penguin Ireland, 25 St Stephen's Green, Dublin 2, Ireland (a division of Penguin Books Ltd)
Penguin Group (Australia), 250 Camberwell Road, Camberwell, Victoria 3124, Australia
(a division of Pearson Australia Group Pty Ltd)
Penguin Books India Pvt Ltd, 11 Community Centre, Panchsheel Park, New Delhi – 110 017, India
Penguin Group (NZ), 67 Apollo Drive, Rosedale, Auckland 0632, New Zealand
(a division of Pearson New Zealand Ltd)
Penguin Books (South Africa) (Pty) Ltd, 24 Sturdee Avenue, Rosebank, Johannesburg 2196, South Africa

Penguin Books Ltd, Registered Offices: 80 Strand, London WC2R ORL, England

www.penguin.com

This collection first published 2011
1

This collection copyright © Hans Ulrich Obrist, 2011
The acknowledgements on pp. 109–10 constitute an extension of this copyright page
All rights reserved

Set in 11/13 pt Bembo Book MT Std
Typeset by Jouve (UK), Milton Keynes
Printed in England by Clays Ltd, St Ives plc

ISBN: 978-0-241-95754-7

www.greenpenguin.co.uk

Penguin Books is committed to a sustainable
future for our business, our readers and our
planet. This book is made from paper certified
by the Forest Stewardship Council.

Contents

Preface by Hans Ulrich Obrist   vii

INTERVIEWS

Digital Architecture : Analogue Architecture   1

Sustainability – A Post-Olympic Interview   25

The Many Dimensions of Ai Weiwei   41

The Retrospective   71

Mapping   101

Acknowledgements   109

Preface

I first came across the work of Ai Weiwei in the second part of the 1990s. While preparing our exhibition *Cities on the Move*, Hou Hanru and I were staying at the Swiss Embassy in Beijing, with the then ambassador Uli Sigg. Uli Sigg is a great patron and collector of contemporary art. The embassy was full of Chinese artworks. Since then I have met Ai Weiwei many times and we have regularly done interviews over a period of ten years. Ai Weiwei keeps extending the notion of art: he is an artist, a poet, an architect, a curator, an expert on antique Chinese craftwork, a publisher, an urbanist, a collector, he has his own blog, and so on. The parallel realities in his work are very complex, and this is what makes him so unique.

Ai Weiwei was born in 1957, the son of the poet Ai Qing, who is regarded as one of the greatest modern Chinese poets. In 1958 Ai Qing was accused as being anti-communist, forbidden to write and exiled to Xingjian province, where Ai Weiwei then spent his youth. Later he moved to Beijing and learned drawing from banned artists who were his father's friends. Drawing became a daily practice then, and still today most of his ideas are fixed with quick sketches. In the late 1970s he participated in a group of young artists in Beijing in an attempt to gain greater personal and artistic freedom. In 1982 he decided to leave China and move to New York. Ai became a friend of the beat poet Allen Ginsberg and immersed himself in the art scene. This is when he abandoned painting and realized that as an artist he could use every kind of object and medium. He turned to photography, capturing political issues like the diaspora of Chinese artists in New York. He also made his first installations in New York.

In 1993 his father became very ill, and Ai Weiwei returned to China; Ai Qing died in 1996. In his artworks Ai Weiwei then began to reflect on the tension between traditional culture and fast-changing modernity. And, as no institutions for contemporary art existed, he also became active in the constitution of an art scene: he published the *Black, White* and *Grey* books (1994, 1995, 1997), which presented interviews with and artworks by Chinese contemporary artists; these books were a kind of manifesto of Chinese avant-garde art. He also curated exhibitions and founded the alternative art space, the China Art Archives and Warehouse in 1997–8. Before that, art was predominantly shown in hotels, apartments and framing shops.

In 1999 Ai Weiwei built his own studio in the north of Beijing. One source of inspiration had been a book on the house that the philosopher Ludwig Wittgenstein built for his sister in Vienna in 1928. Ai Weiwei designed the studio himself only for practical reasons, but as it was widely acclaimed for its unique use of simple structures and materials, it soon triggered an additional career for Ai Weiwei as an architect, in which he has realized over fifty projects. Since he co-designed, with Swiss architects Herzog & de Meuron, the Olympic stadium in Beijing (2008) he is also one of China's most famous architects. In his art and in his architecture he often uses very simple objects and then gives them a new perspective. Ai Weiwei's broad interest in art, architecture and writing reminds me of the great renaissance artists.

In 2006 Ai Weiwei opened up yet another new field and started his Internet blog, which is of outstanding importance, as you will see in these interviews. He was invited to write a blog by a big Internet company that helped him with the technical aspects. The blog soon became a daily notebook, in which he also posted thousands of photographs, documenting his daily artistic and private life – similar to his drawing practice in the 1970s. Over 100,000 people visited the blog every day, until the government shut it down in May 2009. In February 2011 MIT Press published the English translation of the blog. It is a book about life and culture in China. It is about love, sex, identity, interviews, food, the tension between history and modernity, Olympics, music, TV, shopping, death, the government, religion, etc. Ai Weiwei has weaved an unbelievable net of thoughts and words. Blogging produces reality rather than simply representing it. Ai Weiwei is among our very best guides to this new terrain. Over the years all these different activities have become part of Ai Weiwei's extended notion of art. His holistic approach can be compared to that of Joseph Beuys as an interdisciplinary 'social sculpture'.

In our interviews we have talked about all these dimensions of his work as well as what connects them. In their collected form they provide an introduction to the outstanding complexity of Ai Weiwei's artistic thought and work. In one of our interviews Ai Weiwei said about his approach: 'we're actually a part of the reality, and if we don't realize that, we are totally irresponsible. We are a productive reality. We are the reality, but that part of

reality means that we need to produce another reality.'
This is an artistic statement as well as a political one. It
reminds us of the essential need for cultural and political
action in the current situation.

Ai Weiwei has told me that when he was a child his
father had to burn all his books. And when Ai Weiwei
returned to China in 1993, he began immediately producing books like the *Black, White* and the *Grey* books. He has
an affinity for books. This book is published to support
him and to celebrate the many dimensions of his practise.

Hans Ulrich Obrist
London, May 2011

Digital Architecture : Analogue Architecture

While I had known Ai Weiwei since the 1990s as an artist, I was very interested to find that he was also becoming successful for his architecture, when he had always been known for his artistic practice. It seemed an interesting moment, with artists venturing into new fields. I was fascinated by this: how does it work? How does an artist have the ability and capacity to work outside of art?

When I started to see Ai Weiwei more frequently, with Phil Tinari, I realized that it is almost impossible to grasp him in one interview, because he has different studios for different realities: art, architecture and design. Part I of this interview took place in September 2006 at Ai Weiwei's studio home in Beijing. Part II took place in May 2006 and was originally published in the July/August 2006 issue of *Domus* magazine, marking the completion of the Jinhua Architecture Park, a collaborative project organized by Ai Weiwei and his architectural studio.

Part I

HANS ULRICH OBRIST: This is a digital camera.

AI WEIWEI: Yes.

HUO: So you use this camera for your blog?

AWW: Yes, the blog is really a new territory. It's such a wonderful thing. You can talk immediately to people you don't know. You don't know their background and they don't know your background. It's like going on the street and finding a lady on a street corner. You talk directly to her. And then maybe you start fighting, or making love.

HUO: So it's something new for you. When did you start the blog?

AWW: I was forced to start the blog by a company, a big Internet company.* They said, 'Oh, you're well-known, we'll give you a blog.' I didn't have a computer and hadn't done this before. They said 'No, no, you can learn how to do it. We can send somebody to show you.' In the beginning, I put up my old writing and my work,

---

* Chinese web portal sina.com invited Ai Weiwei and a number of other cultural figures, including publisher Hung Huang and developer Pan Shiyi, to begin blogging in late 2005.

then I started to type. I was totally seduced. Yesterday, I put up maybe twelve blog posts after I came back.

HUO: Last night?

AWW: Yes, twelve posts. You can put a hundred photos in one blog entry. People often tell me, 'You have so many photos from one day!' Photos can be anything, about anything. I think that's really information, a free exchange — a careless, responsibility-free solution that reflects my condition very well.

HUO: How many people visit your blog?

AWW: Now, one million some-hundred something. In one day, there are one hundred thousand visitors.

HUO: More than any exhibition ever.

AWW: Yes, ever. I have my opening every minute if I want it. And this is very important to me. If I make art, I make a plan, and people visit the site and come back for half an hour. If I'm lucky, I will make a very good installation for someone I don't know somewhere I don't know, maybe in the Netherlands, Amsterdam. But, with the blog, the moment I touch the keyboard, a girl, an old man or a farmer can read my post and say, 'Look at all this, it's very different, this guy is crazy.'

HUO: It's instantaneous?

AWW: Yes.

HUO: So with this camera you take photographs every-day, wherever you are.

AWW: Yes, whatever the situation. I guess I was over-whelmed because when we grew up we had no chance for any form of freedom of expression. You could even report your father or your mother to the authorities at the worst moment if they said something wrong. This was very, very extreme. Even to this day, people still say you should pro-tect yourself, that you shouldn't say so much in your blog. But I think that everybody has to do things their own way. So far, it's been okay. I often talk about human conditions and social problems in my blog. I think I'm the only one.

HUO: Can we see your blog?

AWW: Yes, I can show you some of the entries. Life in blogs is real because it's your own life, and life is about using time up. It's nothing more than that. It's about how you use it. When I am using it, these one hundred thou-sand people are also looking at my blog. They all spend a small amount of time like I do. A lot of people have said to me. 'Oh, you cannot stop blogging. You should be careful. If they arrest you, what are we going to do?' It's so sentimental – 'We need you; looking at your blog has become a part of our lives.' It's very funny.

HUO: So people care.

AWW: People will wait. If I don't update my blog they will wait the whole night so that they can be the first one to see the new content. They call being the first to comment *shafa*.* So if you are there, that means they are really your fans and they really care what you are talking about. So no matter how late I come home, I always put a few words up there.

HUO: You do this every day?

AWW: I can't tell now when it'll be stopped. Maybe it'll be stopped by authorities. Once, the authorities came and said. 'Hey, we're going to report your blog. It is sensitive. Why don't you take down some pages?'

HUO: This happened?

AWW: They negotiated with me but they were very polite. I said, 'Come on, this is a game. I play my part, you play your part. You can block it if you must because it's very easy for you to block it. But I cannot self-censor, because that is the only reason I have the blog.' So they thought about it and they called me back and said, 'Because of the political situation, we really respect what you are doing.' I think China is at a very interesting moment. Power and the centre have suddenly disappeared in the universal sense because of the Internet, global politics, and the economy. The techniques of the Internet have become a major way of liberating humans from old values and systems, something that has never been possible until today.

---

* Shafa is Chinese for 'sofa'. On popular blogs such as Ai Weiwei's, many readers compete to leave the first comment on new content, usually an exclamation of 'shafa', as if the commenter were the first in a room to sit down on a couch.

I definitely think technology created a new world because our brains, from the very beginning, are based on digesting and absorbing information. That's how we function, but, in fact, conditions start to change and we don't even know it. Theory always comes later. But these really are fantastic times.

HUO: Right now?

AWW: I think right now is the moment. This is the beginning. We don't know what it is the moment of, and maybe something much crazier will happen. But, really, we see the sunshine coming in. It was clouded for maybe a hundred years. Our whole condition was very sad, but we still feel warmth, and the life in our bodies can still tell that there is excitement in there, even though death is waiting. We had better not enjoy the moment, but create the moment.

HUO: You produce the moment?

AWW: Exactly. Because we're actually a part of reality, and if we don't realize that we are totally irresponsible. We are a productive reality. We are the reality, but that part of reality means that we need to produce another reality.

HUO: Maybe the blog doesn't so much represent reality but produce it.

AWW: It's true. It's like a monster, it grows. I'm sure, once somebody looks at my blog, they start looking at the world differently without even knowing it. This is why the Communists, from the beginning, really censored everything. They are the sole source of propaganda, and have been very successful at it for the last fifty years. But because of China's opening, and because of the economy of the world, they won't survive. They can't survive, so they have to allow a certain amount of freedom, but this cannot be controlled once it is allowed.

HUO: When you go to the main page of the blog, there is an image of an ox. Maybe you took the picture in Xinjiang It is always the first image you see, kind of like the blog's logo.

AWW: I just changed it. But it was just a wild pig walking on the ground.

HUO: But it might be the blog's icon or trademark to people.

AWW: People used to see a blood-coloured pig heading west with no direction. The picture was up for one year, so I changed it.

HUO: Today?

AWW: Yes. Last night.

HUO: 12 September 2006, the day we record this interview.

AWW: Yes. I changed it to another one, of a cat. Because, in our architectural studio, my staff spend all day trying to make beautiful models, and then, at night, there are eight cats that destroy everything.

HUO: So the cats attack the architectural models during the night.

AWW: Yes, and they are the only thing better than our government at tearing up the city. But our cats do it faster, and even while we are making plans for the city. It's really a great metaphor for us because we, as a people, love architecture and design. We try to change the world and try to build new models that, at night-time, are always torn up by these cats. These are all beautiful things for their pleasure.

HUO: Cats are architects, urbanists?

AWW: Yes, they are. Cat urbanists.

[Conversation moves to another room, where AWW shows HUO some new works of art.]

AWW: That's what I did last night. I was up until three.

HUO: So this is a new ceramic series you made?

AWW: Yes, ceramics is kind of crazy. I hate ceramics . . . but I do it. I think if you hate something too much, you have to do it. You have to use that.

HUO: To exercise.

AWW: Right.

HUO: And all these boxes, are they architectural maquettes?

AWW: They're full of vases. [Opens one of the boxes and displays a vase.] These are three- to five-thousand-year-old cultural art objects. Just dip them into this house paint, and then they're called coloured vases.★

HUO: The series is called *Coloured Vases* and each vase is different?

AWW: They're all different. On this vase, you can still see old painting on the surface here. And the wall down there is a series that I'm doing, a series of coloured Neolithic rocks. They can be five thousand to ten thousand years old.

HUO: I've heard a lot about the Museum of Modern Art's visit to your home. Who were they, and can you describe what exactly happened?

AWW: It was a big group with the top collectors, top people. On 20 May, MoMA's international council sent sixty or seventy people to China to do a survey of contemporary art. The day they came, this place became stuck on the cultural map.

HUO: Does everybody visiting Beijing's art community come to your studio now?

AWW: Yes, everybody comes, like a tourist shop – you have to go because it sells ginseng or something. It's really

★ In this *Coloured Vases* series, Ai Weiwei dips Neolithic urns into vats of industrial paint, at once destroying their antique and cultural value and transforming them into works of contemporary art.

good for your health or longevity or something. The groups come here on their way to the Great Wall. The MoMA group came on the anniversary of the day in 1942 that the Communists had a meeting at the end of the Long March. It was interesting. They had a monumental meeting on literature and art at which Chairman Mao gave a speech. Today, that speech is still the official bible for Communists.★

HUO: Was that anniversary the exact same day that the MoMA group came?

AWW: The same day. It can't be a coincidence. Everything's related, and, if we can't see how it's related yet, that means that we'll have tighter relationships tomorrow. I said that I should make this anniversary a topic of discussion because, at that time, my father was part of the forum. He was the top literary figure at the time. But, basically, because of the Yan'an forum, art and literature were damaged, and became almost lacking in personal or human conditions, even becoming very brutal later.† Many people have been damaged by the ideas that came out of the Yan'an forums. So we decided to do the only thing that we

---

★ Ai is referring to a speech titled 'Talks at the Yan'an Forum on Literature and Arts', in which Mao declared that art must exist in the service of the people, essentially setting the aesthetic programme for the People's Republic of China.

† Ai's father, the poet Ai Qing, is regarded as one of the finest modern Chinese poets; his poetry is widely taught throughout China today. Despite participating in the Yan'an forums in 1941, he was labeled a rightist in 1957 for criticizing the Communist regime and was subsequently interned in labour camps, first in Heilongjiang, and then in Xinjiang, where Ai Weiwei grew up.

could that day – just record the whole thing but without the group noticing.

HUO: So you used secret cameras to record the MoMA contingent?

AWW: Yes, they were secret because cameras are often used by a group when it wants to monitor another group's activity, as a way of gathering proof. So we filmed them when they went to Factory 798, then we followed their buses from far away when they went to see the artists. Nobody knew. We waited for so long for them to come back. We've even got the driver on tape saying, 'Fuck! It takes them so long just to go to an artist's studio.' Then they drove to my house. The cameras were hidden in the grass so they couldn't see them.

HUO: Small cameras?

AWW: Yes, small cameras. The whole piece is about showing any possible position, recording everyone and not missing anyone so we can identify later who everyone is. It's a very long edit, so I'll just show you a sample. [Shows the video on a laptop.] Here, there is some grass hiding the camera. And they start to study the grass rather than think it has meaning.

HUO: I think the film gives the impression that it's a long visit.

AWW: Yes, these aren't old people but they are all

walking very slowly. It's really according to their movement.

HUO: What do you think the reactions will be?

AWW: About this? I don't know. I can't see the consequences. I just do things without thinking about the before and after.

HUO: You just do it.

AWW: Yes. I don't imagine things. I have no imagination, no memory. I act on the moment.

HUO: The present?

AWW: Yes, the present. Maybe they'll hate it, maybe they'll think it is okay, maybe they'll like it. It's perfect because nobody records it.

HUO: It's a protest against forgetting.

AWW: Maybe their children will buy it or something.

HUO: It's like a portrait of a group in a particular moment in time.

AWW: And there is some kind of suspicious political and cultural condition.

HUO: So this is from yesterday?

AWW: Yes. This guy died thirty years ago, Chairman Mao. It was just the thirty-year anniversary of his death.

HUO: Do you have an archive?

AWW: Yes. I will show you some. These are pictures from last night's party I don't think I have other photos because I didn't stay long enough. The food was okay. [Pointing at pictures on the screen.] That's a famous lady. I left after this food. I had this. This was my dish last night. It was fantastic. These are all yesterday's photos. [Pulling up document on computer.] This is an article about the thirty-year anniversary of the death of Chairman Mao. I am probably going to write about what a criminal he is. It is such a historic situation. And a nation that will not search for its own past and not be critical of it is a shameless nation. We have to work on it. [Pulling up new picture.] This one is very interesting. This is my mother's home in downtown Beijing. Now, Beijing has all been renovated. My home used to have a real brick facade. One day, we went home to see everything had been repainted. So I wrote a blog entry.

HUO: To protest against it.

AWW: Yes, because this is too much. This is a very interesting article. [Displays an article from his blog on the computer.] In just one night, the whole of Beijing was repainted. I wrote a long article. The propaganda slogan for the Olympics is 'One world, one dream.' My article is about how we have lost our homeland and a different world, a different dream. A magazine just called today and told me they want to use it because they love it. They said, 'Can we take out the political part?' Otherwise, it would be impossible for them to print. I said, 'Okay, do whatever you want to. I don't care.' [Shows picture.] This wall was built like a brick. See what they did? They put in concrete. It's amazing! This is private property and they don't even announce the changes. In one day, the whole of Beijing now does not have the same skin as before. Everything is painted.

HUO: Very fast.

AWW: Yes, very fast. It's extremely crazy. This is an amazing photo. This is my home. Now it has become like this. It was real brick. Then they changed the real brick to concrete, and they repainted it. It's amazing. And it's not just my home, the whole of Beijing is going to be like this. There is so much stupidity going on and nobody writes about it.

HUO: So you write about things that nobody else writes about?

AWW: Yes. I mean, what's wrong with this world? Everybody celebrates crazy things. I wrote a blog post about all this, and took photos of how they did it. When I went home, I asked my mum, 'Why did you allow them to do this?' She said, 'Oh, they did it to everybody. What can we do? They said it's good.' I said it's like putting a gold tooth on a mouse. Why did they have to do it? All the fake walls, it's crazy. The old town disappeared in one night. Every door has this. All the doors painted like this. All the windows became like this. It's crazy; it's my home. The doors were made like that so we're taking them down.

HUO: You removed it?

AWW: I removed one piece and I left one piece. So now it's like this.

HUO: Something's missing.

AWW: It became work, protesting. If you totally remove it then there's no memory. But it is related to my work so much that I am happy to substitute.

HUO: It's like a piece.

AWW: Yes, it's like a piece. It's very funny. Everybody touches it and can really see it.

HUO: It would be great to put it in the context of an exhibition.

AWW: People can see it and check on it during the exhibition, every day from Beijing. The title would be the name of my blog. Maybe we can work together on that. Some of it probably needs translating into English. We put some articles in English relating to the city, culture, life, politics, and the environment, anything personal.

HUO: So you agree that we should do this?

AWW: Yes. We will monitor Beijing for you for this show.

HUO: Very exciting. Thank you very much.

Part II

HUO: Over the years you have produced art, architecture, several exhibitions and many publications. In your latest project, the Jinhua Architecture Park, you acted almost as a curator and master planner. Could you tell us a bit about this?

AWW: A few years ago, I was approached by the municipal authority of Jinhua regarding the construction of a park to be dedicated to the memory of my father, who was a well-known poet and intellectual. He was exiled by the Party for political reasons for over twenty years, but was subsequently recognized, after his death, as a major contributor to Chinese culture. When the municipality asked me to oversee the landscaping of this park, at first I refused – I've never been attached to my father's hometown because I grew up elsewhere. But then my mother said, 'If you don't do it, someone else will.' So I went to have a look. The land was an unkempt, two-kilometre-long green strip on the banks of the river Yiwu, but I was fascinated by its position in relation to the city. In the end. I decided to accept the commission.

HUO: You were telling me that idea was essentially to do an exhibition made of pavilions, in which the selection of the architects became an almost curatorial process. The difference is that this is a permanent exhibition, because the pavilions are permanent, aren't they?

AWW: Yes, the pavilions are permanent. We started talking about this project about three years ago. At that time I was working on Beijing's National Olympic Stadium with Herzog & de Meuron, and I asked the municipality if they would be interested in involving them in Jinhua. The planning department responded with enthusiasm. They decided to commission a master plan and a shopping centre for the new Jindong District. In addition, I asked Herzog & de Meuron to work closely with me on the park project. We decided to distribute the programmes that the park required, such as tearooms, bookshops, and toilets, throughout a number of pavilions scattered along the length of the river, and to commission a selection of Chinese and foreign architects to design them. Herzog & de Meuron agreed to design one pavilion and I designed another. Together, we selected a wide range of emergent practices from all over the world to create an interesting and heterogeneous collection of buildings, something quite unique in China.

HUO: So it was a collaboration?

AWW: Yes. I thought it was important to bring as many talented designers as possible into this project. At the moment, China is in desperate need of new ideas, examples of creativity both from inside and outside, and new architectural blood. Conversely, many Western architects are very familiar with architectural theory but don't get many opportunities to build, so this was a welcome occasion to experiment without having to worry about too many constraints. In the end, we invited five Chinese and eleven international practices. In some cases, there were problems with quality control because Chinese builders aren't accustomed to this kind of work, but on the whole the small scale of the projects made it possible to carefully control the quality. Still, we realize now that the project is far more complex than we first anticipated, because when we began we were very naïve and we thought, 'It's a very simple idea.' In general, though, this was a unique occasion for a collective architectural experiment that could have a positive effect on the quality of urban life in Jinhua.

HUO: Where did you study architecture? In recent years your architectural production, especially in Beijing, has been quite prolific. It appears to explore the overlap between Western and Eastern traditions.

AWW: I've never actually studied architecture, although I gained some experience during my civil service. It came later, parallel to my artistic work.

HUO: How did you assign the different programmes to the various architects?

AWW: The first time we all met up in Jinhua for the first visit, we arranged a lottery through which we assigned each practice a different function. From the beginning the meetings were very convivial, almost like parties. Everyone was amazed by the freedom they had to design whatever they wanted, but we had to be very careful with the budget because the municipality didn't have much money. The fact that Herzog & de Meuron were involved also somehow gave the architects a lot of confidence and inspiration. In the end, the municipal authority's strategy was very enlightened, because by allowing this collaboration to go ahead they have attracted a lot of national and international attention to the city. The price of land in the neighbourhood of the park, which until a few years ago was used for agriculture, has risen a lot. A lot of people from universities, journalists, and architects have already come to visit the site.

HUO: Tell me about your own pavilion and its relation to the concept of the archive. It seems like an extension of some of your earlier artworks involving pottery. You did a series of artworks in which you painted with very bright colours some very ancient vases. Somehow you were blurring the boundary between new and old to the point that it became impossible to tell one from the other, right?

AWW: Yes, that's true. In fact, that's the central concept: new or old? Real or fake? These are always the questions that you are asked. It's a theme I often deal with. In any case, the pavilion I designed is an 'archaeological archive'. The city's original commission was for a small museum, but I was more interested in the concept of the archive because I'm an expert on early Neolithic pottery. So this is an archive that can be visited, but it's not simply a container for historical preservation, because some of these vases end up being used in my artworks.

HUO: You keep the vases in your museum but then you might suddenly decide to paint them. It's a sort of museum of artworks in progress.

AWW: Someday I might be tempted to paint the museum,

too, like the pots. When you set up a project like this, all the architects naturally want to do something quite spectacular and striking. I can understand it because they often have so many frustrations in their other projects, and this is an opportunity to challenge conventions. But, personally, perhaps because I'm not solely an architect, I'm more and more attracted to the forms of simple, normal, basic architecture. The shapes that define the 'archaeological archive' are largely derived from local tradition, perhaps simplified even further and transposed into contemporary materials and techniques of production. So the idea is that half of it is above ground, and from this particular angle it looks like a normal house with a pitched roof. From the other side, however, you can see that in fact half of it is submerged – in section, the building is hexagonal. The pathways in the forecourt are also hexagonal, in fact. The building is a single long slab, cast in reinforced concrete.

HUO: Like Herzog & de Meuron's pavilion?

AWW: Theirs is called the Reading Room, and it's composed of a series of folded planes that intersect and slice through each other. Technically, it was very difficult to achieve the form they designed because of the complexity of the mould. They really took advantage of the fact that they were working in China, where labour costs are so low, because the amount of time it took to achieve that form would have been way over budget in Europe. Also, not many people know how to create such a complex but precise sequence of casts: the only person in Jinhua who could do it was an elderly craftsman who had already retired. We had to convince him to start working again, but in the end I think he enjoyed it. He's very proud of having made something that complicated.

HUO: Were all the pavilions realized or did you have any unrealized pavilions?

AWW: They were all realized in the end. At the moment, they are about ninety-five per cent finished. We need approximately one more month to finish the interiors. Money is always lacking, which is why it took us more than a year and a half.

HUO: A year and a half is pretty fast.

AWW: For China, a year and a half is an eternity. We had planned to be finished in four months. But, even though this was a very quick project, I think it will have a big impact in this country. I think architecture can have huge educational value. It tells people about possibilities, and the way things can be changed, and that's always on my mind. It is very important that the government, who financed this project, did something to show that society doesn't have to be all the same all the time.

HUO: What are your plans for the coming years? Will you return to art?

AWW: No, not art. Maybe I'll just read books. I've been thinking of doing some new books myself. You know, I've done a lot of publishing in the past. I had an idea for a book documenting contemporary Chinese art in its early stages, the early 1990s. My three earlier books turned out to be very influential and were crucial in promoting conceptual or experimental art in China, so I think maybe the time has come to do something like that again.

Sustainability – A Post-Olympic Interview

I've been inspired by the model of David Sylvester, the influential British critic and curator of modern art who had an 'infinite conversation' with Francis Bacon, to conduct sustained interviews with artists. The 'infinite conversation' is a recurrent interview offering continued dialogue; it offers us the chance to explore all the aspects of an artist or other inspirational figure.

The post-Olympic marathon, which began with this interview with Ai Weiwei, was part of our marathon series of interview events that started in 2005. The first London marathon was in 2006 at the Serpentine Gallery, with Rem Koolhaas, when Julia Peyton-Jones and I invited him and Cecil Balmond to design the Serpentine pavilion. Since then eighteen marathons have happened worldwide.

Almost everyone in the Chinese art world did something during the Olympics – projects, exhibitions, and so on. It's interesting, in an event-culture world, to think about sustainability and legacy. What do these events really mean in terms of their longer-term improvement of or impact on the culture? We decided to create an inter-disciplinary knowledge festival to reflect on the post-Olympic moment in China, so with Zhang Wei and Hu Fang in Beijing we created a mini-marathon of interviews and discussion. It happened on the last day of the Olympic year, on the eve of a new year.

HANS ULRICH OBRIST: It's incredibly exciting to start this Mini-Marathon with Ai Weiwei. It's not the first time we've spoken, we've recorded interviews on many previous occasions. I want to start by asking Ai Weiwei to tell us his feelings about this very end of the year 2008 in Beijing, and about this post-Olympic moment.

AI WEIWEI: It's my privilege to join this interview, on the last day of 2008, and as the first being interviewed. You asked me about the post-Olympic period: I do have a clear feeling about the Olympics, as a Chinese living in Beijing. But saying too much about it is meaningless. We are living in an era in which nothing is clear, and a social situation that's most primitive, in which the individual still cannot express his or her will. Communication in its most public sense, and discussion concerning the most fundamental questions, are impossible. Everyone, artists in particular, should think about why even today, in 2008, after the Olympics, the Chinese are still stuck in such a situation. If artists betray the social conscience and the basic principles of being human, where does art stand then? So I think 2008 was year one of defending our rights, a year people began to wake up. I believe that the Chinese will face more severe problems in 2009. If our system refuses to communicate, rejecting the idea that everyone is born equal, why should we accept such a system? This is a question everyone must ask. You would be an idiot if you didn't, and can get out of here right now.

HUO: Ever since I left Switzerland many years ago, at the end of my adolescence, my parents would cut out the articles from the newspaper of their small Swiss village, and give them to me at the end of the year. It was always an interesting exercise, because we could see what reaches a tiny village from our global art world. When I was growing up and into the 1980s, there was a lot of reporting about Joseph Beuys and his 'social sculpture', and other very big projects, like the *Last Supper* by Andy Warhol; but in the last couple of years one of the only things that reached the little village were auction records. Now, one exception is Ai Weiwei, not only his project at the last *Documenta*, which travelled far beyond the art world, but particularly your blog. Before we started the marathon, a gentleman approached you from the audience and said he was very surprised that your blog is not shut down. I always thought of the blog as one of the 'social sculptures' of the twenty-first century, so I want to ask you about how the blog started, about your daily practice of the blog, and about how you see it functioning in the current moment.

AWW: My blog is not that much different from anyone else's. Only I am rather continuously paying attention to certain issues that attract my personal concern. These issues are mostly about artists' rights of expression, and the ways personal rights are expressed. In a society like China's, any issue concerning the rights and ways of expression unavoidably becomes political. So I naturally became a political figure. I don't think there's anything wrong with it, because we were born in such a time and we need to face our own problems honestly. Exactly why my blog is still safe at this moment is not something I am in a position to know. I think all danger comes from times and places unknown to you. So I can't speculate.

On how I started writing the blog: I don't think there's anything worth talking about. It's the same old story, you started doing something, and found it presenting lots of possibilities. I think the Internet and information era is the greatest period mankind has encountered. Thanks to this period, humans finally have the opportunity to become independent, to acquire information and communicate independently. Although such information and communication is still restricted and incomplete, compared with the past, people are granted more possibilities to be independent.

HUO: Can you relate to us a few examples of recent entries on the blog. I remember that when I was in China last time, you had protested against the government's repainting the door of your mother's house, then you went back and reinstalled it, so I'm curious what's on right now.

AWW: Let's briefly talk about one or two examples. Of course this year is the most eventful year for China. In the beginning of the year, we went through snow storms, the Wengan unrest, followed by Tibetan unrest, the Sichuan earthquake, and the Olympics. Of course there is one additional case to which I paid special attention, the Yang Jia case.* Thanks to the attention of blogs, this personal case became very public, making it possible for many people to carefully review the judicial system in China, and the legitimacy of procedure. Of course the result is an unfortunate one, but the procedure was indeed clear. Yang Jia's ashes haven't been returned to his mother even today, more than one month after his execution. And his mother was hidden in a mental institution by the police under a false name, Liu Yalin, claiming that she was suffering from a mental disease. This happened in Beijing, during and after the Olympics. It is unbelievable that such an event happened in China. Because we always thought the Chinese Communist Party to be a righteous one, such a thing couldn't happen in China, it seemed plain impossible. However, I have heard about many similar cases now, of people appealing to higher authorities or dissidents being pm into mental facilities. I think this was beyond my wildest imagination.

HUO: Most recently you addressed another public, those affected by the 2008 tainted milk scandal; it would be great if you could tell us about the object you brought with you for the Mini-Marathon Shop. I think it has some particular significance.

AWW: According to the request of the shop, I should bring something. So I bought a bag of Sanlu milk powder from the Internet; I got it from the online shopping website Taobao, and it seems it's for adults. It appeared that

* Yang Jia was a Beijing man executed in 2008 for killing six Shanghai police officers, and whose trial caused a national controversy in China.

the shop owner only had ten bags and could just sell four. Later the price flew very high; this one knows how to do business, very interesting [audience laughs]. The first page of this morning's *Beijing News* said the two alleged perpetrators stood trial in Shijiazhuang city. One of them is a driver. From this, we see in such a case that, after more than 200,000 children have been harmed and the credibility of the entire society has been jeopardized to the greatest extent, the government could still be free from liabilities. And the liability ends up on a driver; I found the event hilarious.

HUO: To come back to your blog, when we spoke last time and I asked you if you were optimistic, you replied that you're very optimistic because of the Internet, that you felt the Internet was the most wonderful thing that could have happened, because somehow it created a rupture with the old value system, and introduced a new value system into the world. So far the art world has used the Internet much less than the music world, where it has become an integral part of almost every release of a record and of dissemination of sound. One could even say that the artworld has been more defensive in its relationship to the Internet. I was wondering if you could tell us a little bit more, also beyond the blog, how you see the future of art and the Internet, and if you think there is viability in the idea of the galleries of the future being online.

AWW: Sorry, all I said just now was about politics. Even I found myself quite cynical. But since you asked such questions, I had to answer. Now we finally come to the questions about the future of art. I think that art won't have too grand or too much of a future if it fails to connect with today's lifestyles and technologies. And all those paintings and sculptures in the past are just very old memories; the people who are attached to the past can still be interested in them. But I believe that, thanks to the possibilities provided by computer technology and communication, great changes have taken place in art in this new era. And the changes will continue more extensively, and more aggressively, in the future. I think that, since these new methods of communication and production will bring us greater pleasure, the bullshit schools such as the Central Academy of Fine Arts in Beijing or China Academy of Art in Hangzhou will no longer be needed. Those most awful teachers learned to mess their brushes around in some really ugly colours, paint some truly horrible paintings with them, then got such prices in the auction houses! I think it's very humiliating, a basic criterion of the unenlightened era of human beings. So I believe such a time will end very soon.

HUO: This idea of the blog as 'social sculpture' is something we also discussed in relation to your collaboration with Herzog & de Meuron to realize the Olympic stadium. Recently you discussed the project with Jacques Herzog and Bice Curiger in an issue of the Swiss magazine *Parkett* [no. 81], in which Herzog said you and he originally conceived the stadium as a public sculpture, a sort of urban landscape, where everybody could climb up and down, meet and dance, do all those fantastic things that people never do in a Western city; he also mentioned that the Eiffel Tower became more successful after the World Expo. You agreed with Herzog that you felt it would be better used after the Olympics, because it would be a more democratic use of the design. As we are here in this post-Olympic moment, I was wondering if you could tell us how you see the use of the stadium now and if it fulfills your expectations so far, and how you see it changing over time?

AWW: I think it's a stadium for a grand sporting event. We first participated in the design process hoping the Olympics could stimulate reform in China, that it would allow China to really join the same conversation, the same value system as the rest of world. But what happened in the Olympics made us realize that it wasn't only different from what we first imagined, but that it was even a set-back, because China became like a police state during the Olympics. Beijing citizens' activities were under severe restriction. There's no point saying too much about it, it's in the past now. As for the 'Bird's Nest', it's a facility of a city, a component of the urban design plan; its future functions obviously are more important than the Games. Its connection with the city, and its physical function and the spirit it represents, should be more important. Of course we can't hope too much, but I hope that, one day, it could really have a chance to become a place represent-ing civil society, a place in which citizens can celebrate.

HUO: This idea of a stadium being not only architec-ture but being urbanism leads us to the question of Beijing. The marathons always have to do with the cities in which they take place, and try to trace out a portrait of the city. I'm wondering if you could tell us your view on Beijing as a city in 2008, because it's the city in which you are working, the city that you've been mapping with your extraordinary video work. It would be great if we could hear more from you about Beijing.

AWW: Beijing is a very big city, with a population of 17 million and maybe a lot of migrants. However, Beijing is the most inhuman city that I have ever lived in, even among Chinese cities. Of course there's nothing wrong with this. Since we are an inhuman society, we should have such an inhuman city. It serves our society well. Besides, my relationship with the city is not that complicated. I may have gone into the city less than ten times this year – five, if I exaggerate a bit. I never went into the Olympic stadium after its completion. At least recently, I don't want to go into that place, so I can't say much more on this topic.

HUO: Stefano Boeri, the chief editor of *Abitare* magazine in Milano and an Italian urbanist and architect, has always said it's impossible to make a synthetic image of a city because a city is too complex; it always escapes us when we try to map it. That similarly mirrors what the painter Oskar Kokoschka said of the impossibility of making a portrait of the city; by the time we grasp one aspect, the city has already changed. I'm very curious about this idea of portraits of cities; you have done these strong video works about Beijing, and I want to ask you to tell us how you map Beijing with these video works.

AWW: I made four videos of the city. The Academy of Arts and Design of Tsinghua University in Beijing invited me to teach a graduate class. Since I never finished school myself, I always felt rather inferior in school. I said that I would teach the class only if I got to choose how I taught. They agreed. I said that I would rent a bus and give classes on the bus. So my students and I spent sixteen days on the bus. We made a plan, and divided Beijing into sixteen parts. Each day, the bus would go through all the streets in one of the sections of the city. The assignment was to do something concerning the city and the moving bus. I put a video camera in front of the bus. In those sixteen days, I completed a 150-hour-long video. Basically, the camera serves like a monitor and is constantly moving forward. And that's the work *Beijing 2003*. It's a visual map of Beijing, recording every hutong* and street that cars could reach. Of course, during and after the recording, the city and its streets had already changed or disappeared. Besides that, I made another one called *Chang'an Street*. From East Chang'an Street to West Chang'an Street, the distance between the east and west perimeters of the Sixth Ring Road is 43 kilometres. I took a one-minute video every 50 metres within those 43 kilometres. So connecting them all made a video a little longer than 10 hours. It records the complete Beijing, from the rural area, to the commercial district, to the political centre Tiananmen Square, then through Xidan, ending at Capital Steel. Then I made *Second Ring* and *Third Ring* immediately following that. There are more than thirty pedestrian walkovers on the Second Ring. I shot one minute of video in both directions of each bridge, making 60 minutes all together. There are more than fifty bridges on the Third Ring Road,

---

* Hutongs are the narrow alleyways between the courtyard houses characteristic of 'old Beijing'.

and I shot the video the same way. The difference between *Second Ring* and *Third Ring* is this: I shot all Second Ring Road ones on cloudy days, and the Third Ring Road ones on sunny days. You can tell it's the Second or the Third Ring as soon as you turn on the video. It's a very phenomenological record I made about the city. But it's a very honest one.

HUO: The other day speaking with Rem Koolhas he suggested that as the city becomes more and more a controlled space maybe the future becomes the countryside – maybe there are more possibilities there. I was wondering if you agree with that. Is the future the city, or is the future the countryside, or both?

AWW: Maybe for Koolhaas the future is in the rural area. But I think the city is still the future of humanity. I think the city provides more powerful possibilities and convenience for the human being. Of course, the information era may relieve such phenomena. But, for the sake of efficiency and due to the extent of humanity's craziness, people can't live without the city.

HUO: That leads us to the question of your manifesto, because earlier this year we conducted a manifesto marathon at the Serpentine Gallery; unfortunately, you had other commitments that day, and couldn't make it to London. Ever since, I have been curious about what might be your manifesto for the twenty-first century?

AWW: The question is a bit grand. To be frank, I can't say too much on this issue, since I feel that it's difficult for us to get something like the most basic needs and most fundamental dignity. So I really can't answer this question.

HUO: I was reading your conversation with Jacques Herzog, and in it you and he were talking a lot about the projects for Beijing and elsewhere that hadn't happened. I was wondering if you could tell us about your unrealized projects: projects too big to realize, too small to be realized, dreams, utopias?

AWW: Of course, as everyone else, I have things on my plate that need to be finished. In 2009, I will have four solo exhibitions. It's very weird for me, since my first solo was in 2004. And there are four very large exhibitions next year, with a combined area of nearly 10,000 square metres. It makes me seem very busy. In fact, I still think those are activities within the old art framework. Of course, I still enjoy my blog. From six to eight this morning, I already wrote two blog entries before my colleagues came to work. I find it more interesting. I am wondering whether I will ever get the opportunity to give up everything else and only write blogs? I found out that I am quite attracted to those very small joys. It gives me pins and needles every day.

HUO: We spoke about art, architecture, and your blog. In our last interview we talked about your relationship to literature, yet we have not talked about music. Dan Graham always said that when we interview artists it's important to know what kind of music he or she listens to, so I want to ask you what kind of music you listen to?

AWW: It's a shame that this last question is the question I find most difficult to answer. Because I was never turned on by any music in my life. I am the one having the least to do with music. Of course, I am able to enjoy music, to be touched. But I never intentionally ask for any music. So for me, the best music should be silent, is mute.

HUO: To end his interviews, James Lipton in *Inside the Actor's Studio* always asks several recurrent questions. You already answered the question of what's your favourite sound – silence – so what's your least favourite sound?

AWW: The least favourite one is the silent music being interrupted.

HUO: What is your favourite word?

AWW: Freedom.

HUO: What's your least favourite word?

AWW: Maybe my name. [The audience laughs.]

HUO: What gives you a buzz?

AWW: I don't want to tell you. Because I don't want to share my buzz with you. [The audience laughs.]

HUO: What irritates you more than anything else in the world?

AWW: Can't find the toilet when I need to go. [The audience laughs.]

HUO: What's the moment we are all waiting for?

AWW: The moment we least want.

HUO: What would have been your dream job?

AWW: Interviews. [The audience laughs.]

HUO: What would have been the job you hated most?

AWW: The end of interviews. [The audience laughs.]

HUO: If God exists, what would you like Him or Her to say to you at the pearly gates? It's the question that Al Pacino answered with 'rehearsal at three'.

AWW: How did you end up here? [The audience laughs.]

The Many Dimensions of Ai Weiwei

When Elena Ochoa Foster opened her exhibition space in Madrid, she invited me to work with her and Ivory Press on a book about Ai Weiwei. We decided to produce a book showing all the facets of his complex practice. For this reason, the title of the book is an homage to Alexander Dorner's *Ways Beyond Art*. A visionary German curator, Dorner ran the Hanover Museum in the 1920s and 1930s. In exile he wrote *Ways Beyond Art*, arguing that in order to understand the forces effective in visual art you have to understand the forces at work in science, literature, architecture and so on, which is exactly the drive behind Ai Weiwei. We wanted to make a book which would, for the first time, bring together all the elements of Ai's work, so the interview that follows tries to grasp the many dimensions of Ai Weiwei.

HANS ULRICH OBRIST: Can we talk about your drawings in relation to your installations and architecture? I thought it would be revealing to publish a series in this Catalogue, to give an idea of them.

AI WEIWEI: There's always a drawing that follows from the initial concept, but I don't keep most of them – they're just thrown away. I do still have some, following on from the architecture projects or installations, and also some models. We have all the drawings for the large installations, and I sometimes use models as drawings. Some we even made after the project. Of course, we did sketches before it was made, but we also did some afterwards. We make a lot of computer drawings for each installation. One person takes over a year to make the drawings, because the process is so complicated. To me, the computer drawings are interesting because they're so precise and detailed. I have made a book from the fragments of all my drawings.

HUO: So there is a book of your drawings?

AWW: Just of one project – *Fragments* (2005).★ It contains

★ Ai Weiwei, *Fragments Beijing* (paperback 2006), eds. Ai Weiwei and Chen Weiqing.

over a hundred drawings. The piece consists of 174 elements, and each element has drawings of its façade and its sections. They can be given to anybody and the object can be produced precisely.

HUO: It can be used like a manual?

AWW: Exactly.

HUO: There are two types of drawings – hand drawings and computer drawings. Do you continue to make the hand drawings even now that you're using the computer?

AWW: The hand drawing continues because there's so much feeling in it: it's kind of classic. You can't take that away. So many artists appreciate that quality. Every time you make a work, you have to do drawings when you discuss the idea with your team. Or, before the concept even comes out, you have to make drawings to illustrate it. I could find some that we could publish. It's a good idea because people are always more focused on the final product.

HUO: And not on the process.

AWW: Yeah, not on how it started.

HUO: So is drawing part of your daily practice?

AWW: No. I blog. The blog* is like my drawing. I read

* http://blog.sina.com.cn/aiweiwei

my e-mails, I write, I take photos. I used to draw a lot. I drew in the train station for months. I have tons of those drawings.

HUO: Made in the train station?

AWW: Yes. In the train station in Beijing, in the late 1970s, before I even got into the university; it was a kind of training. I even drew in the zoo.

HUO: Do you still have those early drawings?

AWW: Some, maybe. My mum threw some away — bags of them — but maybe I can still find a few early ones.

HUO: It's fascinating that you say that your blogs are your drawings.

AWW: The blog is the modern drawing. Whatever I say there could be seen as part of my work. It gives the most information: it shows my complete surroundings.

HUO: I never see you without your camera, which you use all the time to take the daily photos for the blog. How did the blog start?

AWW: It started by coincidence. The Sina Corporation had a plan to set up blogs for a group of people. I told them that I had never used computers, and I didn't know how to operate them. But they said, 'We can teach you.' So I thought about it and I realized that it was the best way to have immediate contact with reality and also to throw my private life out into the open, out to the public. I thought that this was something that had never happened before, and so I decided to try it. In the first blog, I said that the experience itself was the goal – it didn't need to have another aim. Now that you have this technology, you can use it directly – even, to a degree, without thinking about it, without making sense of it. I think that's something that's only possible today. If it had happened earlier, then you wouldn't have seen drawings by Leonardo da Vinci or Degas. I think they'd all have had cameras. My blog is probably the most image-loaded blog internationally; nobody else puts up as many photos each day.

HUO: How many do you take?

AWW: From one to five hundred photos a day.

HUO: Amazing!

AWW: We've taken hundreds of thousands of photos for the blog.

HUO: Do you remember the first thing you put on your blog?

AWW: The first thing was just one sentence. I said something like, 'You need a purpose to express yourself, but that expression is its own purpose.' It was like the idea that you jump into the water in order to survive in there.

HUO: And you just used that, with no image?

AWW: The first one had no image. At the very beginning, you hesitate, you make a careful choice: you think about it.

HUO: The first sentence is really important: it's like a motto. And that was in big letters?

AWW: Yes. You really struggle about why you need to talk to other computers like this. You ask yourself the best way to make this virtual reality public through cybertechnology. It's kind of weird at the beginning. It's like if you throw something into a river: it immediately disappears, but it's in there and it changes the volume of the river, depending on how many objects are thrown in. I think 19 November was the first day of my blog; it's been almost three years now. I've already published over two hundred articles, interviews and writings, commentaries about art, culture, politics, newspaper cuttings, etc., on it. I find that this is the most interesting gift to me, or even to China, because we live in a society where self-expression is not encouraged and can even damage you, as it has two generations of writers. People are afraid to write anything down; any words put on paper can be used as evidence of a crime. That's why Chinese intellectuals are so careful now.

HUO: It's interesting that it started with a written line. Last time we did an interview, we talked about your beginnings; we discussed your relationship with your father but we didn't really go into your own writing, and I'm curious about this.

AWW: Yes, I'm also very curious about my own writing. I grew up in a society where to be an intellectual, or to read or to write, was not encouraged. My experience of reading was if I touched a book my father would say, 'Ah, put it down, it's not good for your eyes.' He was just like an old farmer.

HUO: He really thought that way?

AWW: Yes. We were in this really remote village. He did his daily work and he thought that it was not a good thing for his children to read because the future was very clear in China – anybody with knowledge would be punished. You couldn't speak your mind because it could lead to death. So you wouldn't let somebody in your family read. And I have one regret: I feel sorry that I can't write well. That's the skill that I value the most. I think that, if I could write well, I'd give up my art for writing. For me, it's the most beautiful and effective way to illustrate my thinking. When I started this blog, I'd already made up my mind to practise my writing. In the beginning it was difficult, but since then it's improved, and for that I have to thank this technology: it made it much easier for me.

HUO: It liberated your writing in some sense?

AWW: Oh yes, very much so. Now I can easily write one thousand words a day, or in one morning.

HUO: Do you agree that now there's less of a link between art and literature than there was in the early twentieth century? I think that the bridge between art and literature was always the key in the avant-garde – in Surrealism and

Dadaism. I'm curious because I think you've always had this desire to create this link with literature in your art. You were telling me before that you drew cars for Bei Dao's first book. Can you talk about your dialogue with poetry?

AWW: Poetry, of course, has influenced me more than any other writing. One has to remember that, before we burnt all the books during the Cultural Revolution, I had read a few books of poetry, like Mayakovsky in Russian, and Rimbaud and Whitman and Tagore and Baudelaire. Poetry for me is almost like a religious feeling. Sometimes you feel infinity in it. But each poet is different. For example, William Blake, the British poet . . . I remember Allen Ginsberg, who really loved William Blake, used to read his poems to me, and he'd also read his own poems.

HUO: How did you meet all these people? Because on the one hand you had these links, obviously, to your father, and then to Chinese poets of your own generation.

AWW: Through my father. All the poets in China would come to my father. He was somebody who all the poets really liked, and when Bei Dao had just started writing, before he published anything, he'd bring his handwriting to show my father. At that time, I was just eighteen and he was just over twenty and we spent time together.

HUO: And is that when you did the book cover for him?

AWW: Yes. He wanted to make an album of his poetry.

Of course, nobody could print anything like that, but he knew someone, a girl who used to do typing for a military unit. At that time in China, if you could type, your status was very high; your power was secret – you know, public security-controlled – because that meant you were involved in propaganda. Typing was a superior job in Chinese society, and in Russia too. Someone who had access to a typewriter was always busy because of this mysterious situation. Everything had to be typed out ten times, a hundred times, to make copies – there were no photocopy machines. The paper was very rough. The book of poetry was called 陌生的海滩 which means 'Strange Beach'.

HUO: Which poets do you admire today?

AWW: There are some young poets, but these days almost nobody reads poetry.

HUO: We need to bring it back.

AWW: Yeah, yeah. It's crazy. But poetry seems to be appearing through other forms. I once asked Allen Ginsberg, 'Who's the best poet of today, of the younger generation?' He thought about it, and said, 'Bob Dylan'. That was in the 1980s.

HUO: And how did you meet the Beat generation poets?

AWW: I met Allen at a poetry reading in St Mark's Church in New York. Annually we would have this poetry reading. I saw this old man come up and noticed that everybody respected him, and then he read some long poems about China. So I thought this was interesting. When he came down from the stage, he passed me and he realised that I was Chinese and we started to talk and it turned out that he had been to China and met my father. He said that my father had given him the warmest greeting: they hugged each other. Normally Chinese people would just shake hands, but they hugged each other. So he was very affected by that.

HUO: A bit like family.

AWW: Yeah. We chatted for a long time and became very close. He often invited me to give poetry readings, and I remember two Christmases, or New Year's Days, that we spent together. He'd come to my apartment and read his long poems to me. It was very interesting. He had lots of poet friends he sometimes introduced me to: Gary Snyder and many others whose names I don't remember. I also met Robert Frank, the Swiss photographer who did *The Americans*. They were always together.

HUO: And did you ever collaborate with him?

AWW: No, although sometimes he did collaborations. Once he gave me a book that he'd collaborated on with the artist Hermetti. Hermetti made illustrations and paintings for his poetry.

HUO: How would you define poetry?

AWW: I think that poetry is for keeping our intellect in the stage before rationality. It brings us to a pure sense of contact with our feelings. At the same time, of course, it does have a strong literary expression; but the most important thing is that it brings us to the innocent stage in which imagination and language can be most vulnerable and at the same time most penetrating.

HUO: Now I'd like to move on from poetry to something completely different – to architecture. Obviously you're working in the context of contemporary art, but then you also work in all these other contexts. I was speaking the other day to the artist David Hockney, and he was telling me that, whenever he needs to reinvent his painting, he goes into something else: he writes an art history book, or he makes a movie, and then he comes back to art and it gives him new ideas. So, I was wondering whether you consider architecture to be a detour from art, or if it's a parallel reality. I think it's fascinating that you're one of the only artists who's really developed an architecture practice besides their art practice, which isn't just an elusive conception but which is real. And you've actually realized more buildings than many European architects of your generation who've been trying their whole lives to create buildings, yet it doesn't seem to be your main activity.

AWW: It was something I did very unconsciously: to build my own studio and then to build other things. And then gradually some very good architects began to say, 'Hey, we like your work, we think you're really an architect, judging from your control and your way of looking at and dealing with things.' I was surprised. I never felt architecture was a big deal. Maybe it's a kind of poetry to me. You use your hands, and you're dealing with the volume and the size and the loading to illustrate your understanding of art and the human condition. So, it comes naturally to me.

HUO: It just happens?

AWW: I've never had any difficulties. I always think that mankind should have good-quality architecture. You imagine the possibilities and you make it become part of reality. So that, I think, is man's ability, and that's beautiful: you can change your conditions. That's a very essential act.

HUO: In the nineteenth century, Whistler said, 'Art happens.' So one could say in your case that architecture happens. But you didn't study architecture. Were there any architectural influences – Le Corbusier or Mies van der Rohe or Frank Lloyd Wright? Did you have any heroes in architecture?

AWW: I had one influence in architecture, if I can call him an influence. At that time, I was in Wisconsin with a group of young Chinese poets. I was accompanying them on a poetry-reading tour, and I went to a bookstore and I found a book called *The Wittgenstein House*. You know, the philosopher. He built a house for his sister, in Vienna. And so, because I like his writing, I was fascinated by the book, and the building was absolutely great. From the larger concept to the details – like door handles and heating elements – it was all designed by him, and he was so precise, and he controlled the architecture so clearly. I heard that, after he'd built it, he wanted to raise the building by a few centimetres, believing that the proportions were slightly wrong. That to me is very interesting. That's what I think architecture is about.

HUO: How very fascinating! Wittgenstein was much more important to you than any other architect?

AWW: Oh, much, much more, and much more important than many, many artists for me. He's so articulate in his expression. He tried to crack the absolute truth there. The effort, the repeated effort, made all his practice become one – just one act. So that for me is the most fascinating thing. I think that part of architecture has never been taught in schools, and that nothing students are taught is as important as this. What he did is absolutely necessary for any good architecture. He said that the way good architects distinguish themselves from bad architects is that the bad architects always try to do everything that's possible while the good ones try to eliminate the possibilities.

HUO: But at that time, were you reading many architecture books?

AWW: At that time, I just had that book. I didn't read it at all. I mean, why should I read an architectural manual? But it was an old book, out of print, so that's why I bought it. That's the only gift I had from architecture when I went back to China. The only architect I could remember was Frank Lloyd Wright, and the reason why I remembered him was because of the Guggenheim Museum, which I often visited. I always thought that it was a problematic museum: you can never hang a painting evenly because

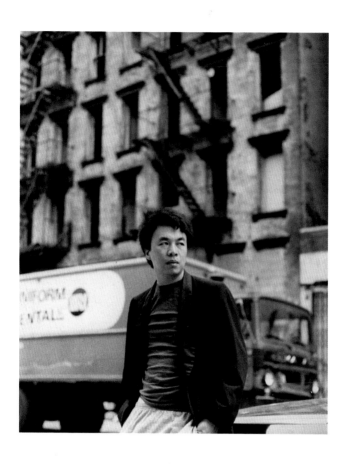

Ai Weiwei in New York's East Village, 1985. Self-portrait.
(photograph: Ai Weiwei)

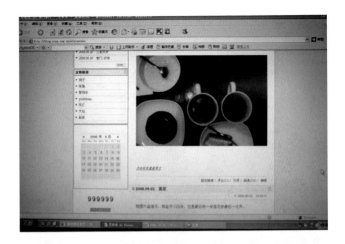

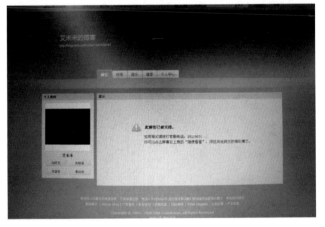

(*top*) Ai Weiwei's blog, which he integrated into his art.
The blog ran from 2006 until 2009.
(photograph: Ai Weiwei (2006))

(*bottom*) Ai Weiwei's blog being shut down.
(photograph: Ai Weiwei (2009))

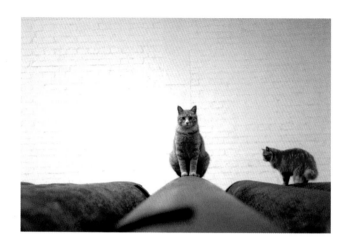

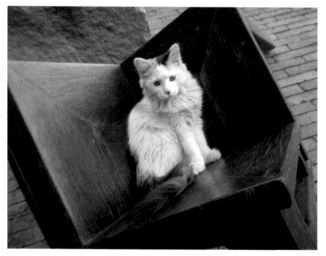

(*top*) Two of Ai Weiwei's cats, resting on beams in his studio.
The image was posted on his blog.
(photograph: Ai Weiwei)

(*bottom*) A cat resting on *Table with Three Legs*.
(photograph: Ai Weiwei)

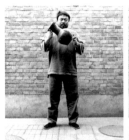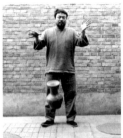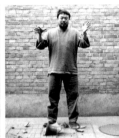

Dropping a Han Dynasty Urn
(Ai Weiwei (1995). Three b/w prints each 148 × 121 cm)

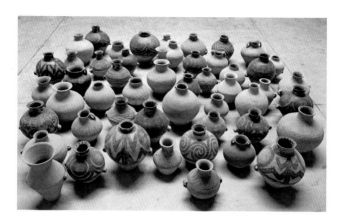

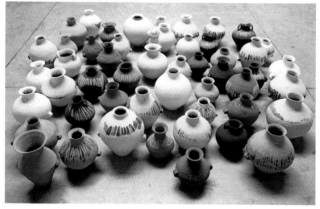

Coloured Vases
(Ai Weiwei (2006). Neolithic vases (5000–3000 BC) and industrial
paint. Fifty-one pieces, dimensions variable)

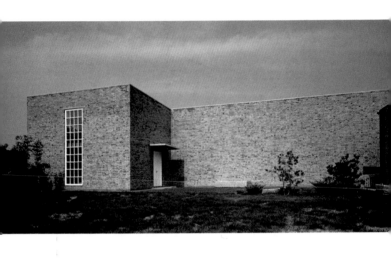

Ai Weiwei's Studio House, Beijing, 1999. Ai Weiwei designed and built this, his first architectural project, inspired by the house that Wittgenstein built for his sister.
(photograph: Ai Weiwei)

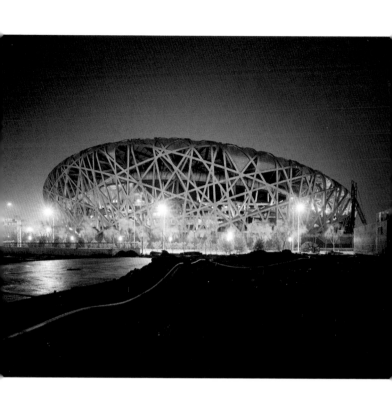

Ai Weiwei worked with the architects Herzog & de Meuron
on China's Olympic Stadium, known as 'The Bird's Nest'.
(Ai Weiwei (2005–8), 100 colour prints, dimensions variable,
100 × 142 cm)

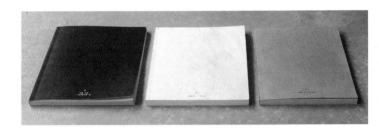

When Ai Weiwei returned to China in the early 1990s, he produced *The Black Book*. Two more volumes were published, capturing China's art scene at that time.

(Ai Weiwei, *The Black Book* (1994), *The White Book* (1995), *The Grey Book* (1997), each 160 pages, 23 × 18 cm)

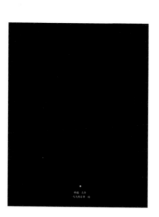

中国文学 北京
一九九五年 试刊

中国文学 一九九六

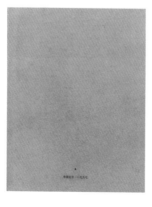

中国文学 一九九七

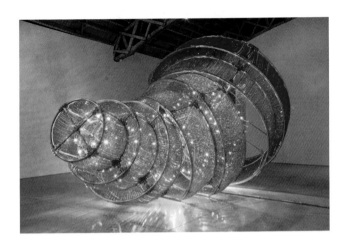

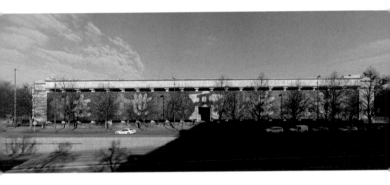

Descending Light
(Ai Weiwei (2007), glass crystal, lights and metal, 400 × 663 × 461 cm. Photograph courtesy Mary Boone Gallery)

Remembering
(Ai Weiwei (2009), backpacks and metal structure, approx. 920 × 10,605 cm. Image courtesy Haus der Kunst, photographer Lawrence Weiner)

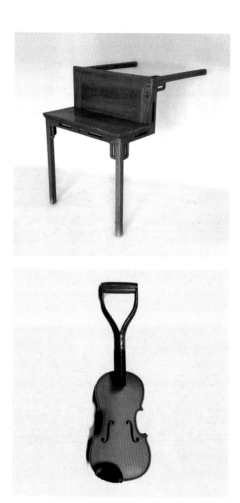

Table with Two Legs on the Wall
(Ai Weiwei (1997), table Qing Dynasty (1644–1911), 90.5 × 118 × 122 cm)

Violin
(Ai Weiwei (1985). Shovel handle, violin, 63 × 23 × 7 cm)

In 2007 Ai Weiwei created *Fairytale* at *Documenta* 12 in Kassel, Germany.

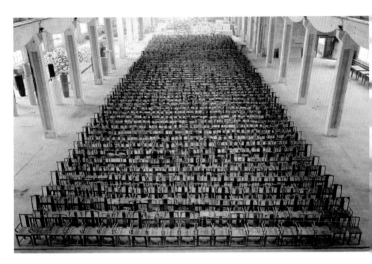

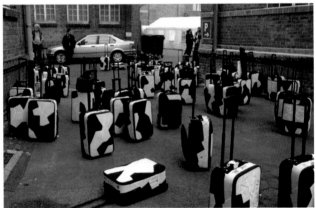

(*top and bottom*) (Ai Weiwei (2007), 1,001 Chinese visitors in Kassel)

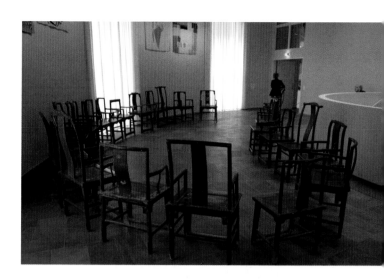

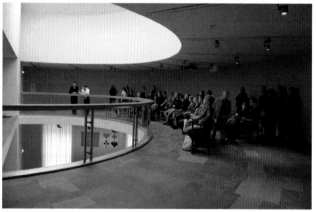

(*top*) Installation view at *Documenta* 12, in Kassel, One
(Courtesy: the artist; Leister Foundation, Switzerland; Erlenmeyer
Stiftung, Switzerland and Galerie Urs Meile, Beijing-Lucerne)

(*bottom*) Installation view at *Documenta* 12, in Kassel, Two
(Courtesy: the artist; Leister Foundation, Switzerland; Erlenmeyer
Stiftung, Switzerland and Galerie Urs Meile, Beijing-Lucerne)

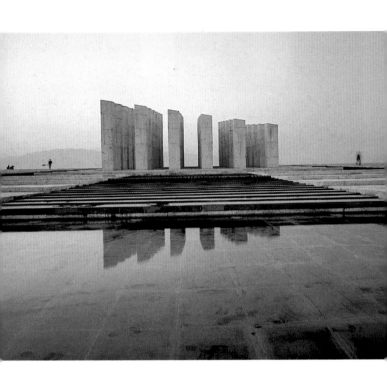

Ai Qing Cultural Park, Jinhua, Jiejiang, China. One of Ai Weiwei's architectural projects.
(Ai Weiwei, 2002–3)

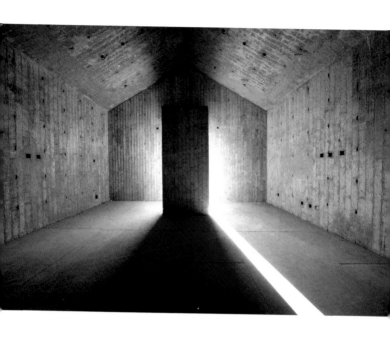

Neolithic Pottery Museum, Jinhua Architecture Park, China;
another architectural project.
(Ai Weiwei, 2005)

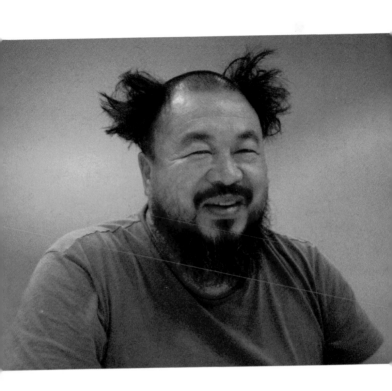

Ai Weiwei, 2006.
(photograph: Ai Weiwei)

the ground isn't flat. But of course, now I think he was very avant-garde to design a museum like that at that time.

HUO: The Wittgenstein house triggered everything, and then you built your own studio, and then it became almost like an avalanche of buildings. And that wasn't planned? There was no master plan – it just happened?

AWW: No, nothing was planned. The most beautiful thing that ever happened in my life was by coincidence and not by plan. And it often happens because you don't plan. If you have plans, you only have one go. If you don't have plans, it often turns out well because you've followed the situation. That's why I've always jumped into unprepared situations, the most exciting conditions.

HUO: How would you describe your architecture? I was reading Svetlana Boym's manifesto last night and she writes about the architecture of adventure and the architecture of threshold and the architecture of subliminal spaces and of porosity and doors and bridges and windows. She writes about Tatlin and other radical experiments with architecture in the historic avant-garde. Do you relate to that? I'm thinking of some of your recent installations, and their ultimate connection to architecture.

AWW: At first, I didn't know anything about it. I kept my innocence through not knowing. Shigeru Ban was the first one to recognize me, and I appreciate that so much. He came to my place because he had to do something in China and he wanted to find out how local people built. And then the developers said, 'Oh no, the artist did his own building.'

So he was introduced to me. He came to my house, and, before he left, he said. 'I think that you're a very good architect.' I was surprised: it was just my studio, which I designed in one afternoon. I made the drawings and the labourers built it in sixty days. I never intended to think for a second about architecture. He said, 'Do you know Louis Kahn's work?' I'd never heard of him – that was in 2001 or 2002 – I said, 'No, I don't know it,' and he shook his head. He thought that I must know this guy. But later I realized he was a great architect. And then he gave some lectures in China, and during a lecture he said that there were no architects in China except one person he knew, whose name was Ai Weiwei: 'I think he's a good architect.' Twice he said that, so everybody in the architectural world was wondering, 'What? Who is this guy?' And many magazines started to ask me for interviews. And he also very generously introduced my work to *a+u*, a Japanese architectural magazine.

HUO: It is a very good magazine.

AWW: They did the first publication of my studio, and that was also the first publication they ever did on Chinese architecture. And then that was followed by a German architectural magazine called *Detail*, which also made a very nice report on my studio. They put it into the tradition of the brick house from Roman times to today. They presented my studio as a living example of the fact that people were still building brick houses. Ha! It was kind of funny. I have so many projects that I must do. But I mustn't plan it. People come to see me and say, 'Can you help?' And so I say, 'Why not?' You can make a little effort to change the conditions.

HUO: Brick plays a role in most of your buildings. Is that a 'Personified Abstraction', as Raymond Hains called Yves Klein's blue, for example, or just a basic element of architecture? Or how you would explain the recurrent use of brick?

AWW: I like to use the most common objects. Even in my art, I use things like shoes or a table. These objects are already cultured – people have already put a lot of knowledge and thought into them. I think I'm dealing with that in the most effective way. And also bricks are still cheap and the easiest part of the building. They have a very natural relationship with our hands, in terms of their size and weight. It's almost like you can build them blindly, or it's like using words to write something – it's very easy. Maybe that's because they're very economical and handy. I also did a concrete building. I think that that's also very essential.

HUO: Not only did you venture into architecture, but you also started to curate. When did you start curating? Was it related to your first space?

AWW: Yes. I did the first art space in Beijing in 1997 at the Chinese Art Archives and Warehouse, and the reason for doing it was that there was no facility in Beijing for showing contemporary art properly. The works had just been shown in hotel lobbies and framing shops. So I thought that it would be very easy to provide a space so that artists would have a chance to see their work in a real contemporary facility for the first time. At that time, I'd already published a few books with artists: *The Black Book, The White Book* and *The Grey Book*.

HUO: It's interesting that from your early experience there's been this idea of the disappearing book: the idea of the destruction of books. Can you tell me about these three books?

AWW: The first one, *The Black Book*, was done in 1994, after I'd come back to China. At first I had nothing to do, and then there were many young artists wanting to come and talk to me. And I thought, 'Why don't we do a book?' There were no galleries, no museums, no collectors and the book could at least record the basic concepts for future study, or as evidence. So I talked to two friends, Xu Bing and Zeng Xiaojun, who also thought that it was a good idea, and so we decided to do it. But they were in the United States so I had to bear the full responsibility. I designed the concept and I found an acting editor, Feng Boyi, to help me. So we designed our first book very quickly. It focused on the concept that the artists should write down what was in their minds rather than painting a canvas or making a sculpture. I remember when they sent me all the materials; they were all photos of their paintings and sculptures. And I said, 'Return all those photos. We don't need any of them. I'm not interested in what you've done, I'm interested in what's in your mind, what's behind those works.' Nobody understood why they had to write it down, and none of them wanted to. So I said, 'No, no, no, to me they're all equally good or equally bad works; there is no single work that's better than the others, except your mind.' So, then they started writing. I said, 'Give me one sentence, one word, but it has to be done by you.' So each of them made some kind of solitary text or poem, or whatever. So it's a book about the mind. We published the first book and it became very popular, we sold three thousand copies. There was nothing else to read! We tried to circulate it underground, and, of course, we got noticed by the Public Security Bureau, and they started asking questions. Then, before it was published, Xu Bing dropped out. He was so scared; he said 'We cannot circulate anything and we shouldn't publish it because this is too dangerous. Later, I want to go back to China to work.' I said to him, 'Sorry, you can drop out, but I will publish it because I made a promise to the artists. I can't self-censor it. If there's a problem, the police can come to me. I'll fully explain my position and I'll take the consequences. But the fact that there's danger isn't enough for me to stop it.' So he dropped out: he wasn't part of the final result. It turned out that we didn't get into much trouble and it became very important at the time. So we published the second volume and the third volume in the following years, and then I stopped because the artists began to print their own catalogues, and the political situation got much looser. There was no longer the need for me to do the book. I always take action when it's needed.

HUO: When it's action, not reaction?

AWW: Yes, and not for any other reason. So I stopped. Then somebody asked me if I could do a show. So I did this show called *Fuck Off* in Shanghai: in 2000 I gathered those people who were in the previous books and some new artists together and made this show. And then I got involved in architecture. People often came to me to ask if I could do this or that, and then I began to query it. I realized that doing it by myself wasn't enough. The projects had to be big and could be much more interesting and could raise public consciousness much more. So I first started curating for the SOHO contemporary city sculpture project: thirteen artists collaborating on a public sculpture project. Each was to contribute one work. It turned out very well and resulted in very fine works. And since then I've circulated and have met many people. When I ask them to collaborate, they respond very carefully. I wanted to do some architecture with Herzog & de Meuron in Jinhua Architectural Art Park. We had the idea to do not just one project, but many small architectural ones at different locations in the city. It would be to stimulate the civic conditions, rather than to build monumental objects. So, to introduce that idea, we decided to ask a group of architects to participate. I curated that one and Jacques Herzog gave me the list of names.

HUO: So that's what led to your curating of architecture?

AWW: Yeah, that was the first one and it turned out very good, because we were not only curating, but were also helping them to build. So the product was rewarding. Recently, a developer asked me to do a big project and I said, 'No, no, no, we're not going to do any big projects anymore, but I will help you curate it.' I think it's a good idea to have more architects involved internationally and for those young architects to have the chance to come to China and to practise their knowledge here and to learn from here. I talked to Jacques and said that I needed one hundred architects. He was shocked, and said, 'What?' And I said, 'Yes, I need one hundred architects.' So they provided me with the names. I think they're from about thirty nations. So we wrote to those architects and immediately we got a response. They all wanted to be involved, all one hundred.

HUO: It'll be one of the biggest forums of architects of our time.

AWW: Yeah, and they're all about the same generation: your age or even younger, and they're the best result of the architectural education over the past ten or fifteen years. So it's really a survey. We had a big meeting and discussion, and they all came with their friends and colleagues – it turned out to be three hundred of them – and they took part in this project. They felt the most exciting part was seeing each other in Inner Mongolia, in China, and working on this strange project where everybody was focused on the same conditions, but with this great variety of backgrounds and education. Many people had heard about each other, had read about each other for quite some time, but would never have had the chance to sit together in one big room and to watch Mongolian dancers while drinking hard liquor at a big party. There was such excitement and craziness. But, for me, it was the most natural, easy act to build up just one condition, to set up a possibility. It doesn't cost me any actual effort and the result is very interesting. So I see myself more as somebody who triggers or initiates things. Also I did *Fairytale* – that was a similar project.

HUO: Can you tell us about *Fairytale*?

AWW: I brought 1,001 Chinese people to Kassel. It came from a very simple idea: I was walking with Uli Sigg in Engadin. There were many people passing by us, and Uli asked me, 'Do you have any idea what you're going to be showing in Kassel?'

HUO: For *Documenta?*

AWW: Yes, at *Documenta*. I said, 'I don't know what I'm showing but I know what I'm not going to show. I'm not going to show a painting or an object or an installation.' 'What are you going to show then?' I saw all these tourists from Milan passing by and I said, 'Maybe I'll bring a lot of Chinese to see the show.'

HUO: So it was in the Swiss mountains that the idea was triggered?

AWW: In the very thin air you see the details . . .

HUO: Yes, in the Engadin Valley at an altitude of two thousand metres the brain works better. Nietzsche wrote in Sils-Maria.

AWW: Yeah, it sort of recycles your brain condition; it's like a drug.

HUO: You also showed a major sculpture in Kassel, but then it collapsed. Can you tell me about this sculpture?

AWW: I told the Kassel curators about what I was going to do. Everybody seemed to like the idea, but at the same time they didn't believe that it was going to happen – that I'd bring a thousand people. And the financial, diplomatic and political conditions were quite difficult; there were a lot of obstacles, So they also asked me, 'And besides that?' So I think that they thought that it wasn't really going to happen. They said, 'We need another outdoor sculpture, the template. We really think that you're the only one who could do it,' so I said, 'Okay.' And they built it. I would never have imagined that there could have been such a storm in Germany – so strong, so severe – which immediately destroyed it. And, after it had been destroyed, I looked at it and I thought it looked really nice, so I said, 'Let's show it this way.' And we decided not to touch it: we just reprinted the postcard. The only thing was, would Germany allow it? This unpredicted, undersigned happening? Others said that Germany would never allow us to do that. But they did.

HUO: And the Madrid exhibition in May will include all the different aspects of your work?

AWW: Yeah, I really love the idea, the very interesting, ambitious concept of this exhibition. It's about how everything relates to each other, yet everything is itself.

HUO: Which installations will you show there?

AWW: There's going to be a Monumental Junkyard, bubbles, marble chairs, a map of China and another large scale woodwork.

HUO: Can you tell me about these bubbles? I saw them in photographs and there was almost something of a scientific experiment about them, and yet they were very solid.

AWW: Yeah, it's true. I was thinking about the high-quality porcelain that was made for the emperors in the old days. It was small in size – glasses, cups and bowls – and the craftsmanship was superb. I was fascinated by how it could be used in Chinese houses, how to take the whole nature of this porcelain production and that kind of skill and tradition into contemporary practice. And that's challenging because the technical process only allows certain things to be done. I have my own kiln and I have over twenty people constantly working there, experimenting and practising. And then a product comes out. I want the size to be more like the scale of furniture, which can be put in any place. You can't identify it; it's not something you're familiar with. It's more like a foreign object because you don't know its usage, but it's made to such high quality that you can't ignore its purpose. But what its purpose is you don't know. I feel it's very interesting to put a tremendous effort or art or craftsmanship into something useless or even nameless. You cannot name it, because when something has never been used, we cannot use it in the future. In a sense, it's not there. Although it's a physical thing, it's not there.

HUO: It's almost in a limbo kind of space, isn't it?

AWW: Yeah.

HUO: And you'll also show *The Wave* if I understand right?

AWW: Yes. I am showing my early ceramic works, and also other objects. I will include photographs of Beijing Airport's Terminal 3, designed by Norman Foster.

HUO: That's another aspect of your work that you haven't talked about: the photographs. You use photographs for the blog, but you also take other photographs.

AWW: Yes. I do take small photographs like a type of evidence.

HUO: Evidence?

AWW: Yeah, they're more like a pure recording: no judgement. They also relate to a group of videos I've been doing since 2003 about Beijing.

HUO: Which I saw in your recent video exhibition in Beijing. For the video *Beijing 2003* you drove around for seven days, didn't you?

AWW: Yes. And the photos are cumulative – a big volume of evidence, of very different aspects. But it's so big, I don't know how many there are.

HUO: How many photos have you taken altogether? Tens of thousands?

AWW: Hundreds of thousands.

HUO: Hundreds of thousands! Leon Golub once told me that it almost becomes organic, like second nature, this idea of so many images.

AWW: Yes, that's right. You also build up your sensitivity to the world. It's like an animal with many,

many antennae. Everyone tries to grab at reality in some way.

HUO: Will you also show *Bowl of Pearls*?

AWW: No, no *Bowl of Pearls*. A vase with a Coca-Cola sign [*Coca-Cola Vase*, 2008].

HUO: What else are you working on at the moment?

AWW: A film about Yang. Today, Yang is in court; it's very interesting. One day he rented a bicycle in Shanghai and was stopped on a street corner by the police to answer questions about the legality of the bicycle. He had an argument with the police, asking, 'Why did you stop me?' and so on. He showed the police the proof of the rental papers and the police were very arrogant and took him to the police station, and then what happened nobody knows. They questioned him and he stayed there until midnight or two in the morning. He claims he was brutalized by the police and became impotent. He complained and filed grievances, and no one responded to them. The police said, 'We didn't do anything wrong, all we did was standard procedure.' But I don't believe it. That wouldn't cause him to come back to Shanghai from Beijing with such anger. He came back and killed six policemen and hurt another five. He ran up twenty-four floors. This has become so sensational because for the Chinese, even just to say 'no' to the police isn't possible, and the police are very brutal and very ruthless. Everybody knows it. The police said that he had done it. Immediately, they tested him, and found that he's not mentally ill, and the police hired a lawyer for him, but the lawyer also had a steady job working for the government. This guy, he's so amazing. He's like a philosopher. They said: 'If you don't remember killing them, then that's because of your attitude. You're trying to ignore the memory.' And he replied, 'No, if I don't remember that only means that I don't remember.' He can memorize like a film so he can tell in great detail what happened. People said that they showed him a video of a person in a mask, running down the stairs, right after the deaths, and he asked the judge, 'How can you prove that it is me wearing a mask?'

HUO: But it was him?

AWW: We don't know. But they have to prove he's guilty. But he's like a lawyer, you know. He is so incredible, so clear. He talks so well. He said, 'Believe it or not. That is your position.' He also said, 'In the videos that person is not me.' And then they found a blog, proof that it was him. But he said, 'No, that's also impossible because I don't have a blog. Where did you find this blog?'

So I recently posted a message on my blog, questioning all those judicial problems, I said, 'Yes, he killed somebody, maybe, but, still, before you prove that he really did it, there are many, many things which we cannot easily believe. Why did he do it? What was the reason for this crime? And if he travelled to Shanghai from Beijing, what's the reason?' The police also mentioned that, because he'd complained, they had come to Beijing twice, and the police also tried to pay him some money but he would never take it. So that raised more questions, because no police would come to another city twice if someone hadn't done anything wrong. Why did they have to come to Beijing twice? Why did they have to pay him damages? So there's definitely something wrong.

HUO: So you're preparing an investigative piece on this?

AWW: Yeah. We're doing a documentary. We did interviews with people. And then his mother disappeared. Nobody knows where she is. So I just asked, 'Where is his mother?' And now it's become a great social issue and the trial has been delayed and delayed until today. Today is the second trial. After the first trial they announced the death sentence, so really he's fighting for his life.*

HUO: So it's today?

AWW: Yeah, right now. From nine o'clock in the morning. I think that the trial has a tremendous problem now because it's not a fair trial, and I don't know how they can continue with this.

HUO: I'd love to see this film. Is it already out?

AWW: No, we are still filming.

HUO: I've got two last questions. Firstly, I want to ask you about nature. You said you had to be Picasso or Matisse to compete with nature. So I was very curious about this idea of competing with nature.

* Yang Jia was executed on 26 November 2008.

AWW: I think that competing with nature is basically a Western idea. As a Chinese, you're always part of your surroundings. Nature can be a man-made or an industrial postmodern society. I believe that you're always part of it and consciously or unconsciously you're in there, trying to build up some kind of relationship, which means the consciousness and awareness will be useful to others. That's our condition.

HUO: And the last question brings us right up to today. We're here on 13 October 2008. It's the moment of the global economic crunch in many markets. And I was wondering how you see the current moment. Are you optimistic?

AWW: In the short term, I think I am very optimistic. Humans only learn from things like this. Basically, humans are monsters; they behave ruthlessly. This period has come, and I think that it's very important for everyone to see that we're entering a new world, a new condition, and a new structure, and to see the possible potential damage. It's a very, very exciting time and I think that everybody will learn something from it.

The Retrospective

In 2006 Markus Miessen and I founded the Brutally Early Club. It's a breakfast salon for the twenty-first century, where art meets science meets literature. We founded it because it's so hard to improvise in contemporary cities, where everybody has a schedule and life is decided weeks in advance. But most people are free at 6.30 in the morning.

In 2009 Phaidon published a full monograph of Ai Weiwei's work. Ai Weiwei and I recorded the following interview for the book. We were both in Dubai for the art fair and decided to have a more retrospective conversation. We also decided to do it Brutally Early.

HANS ULRICH OBRIST: Can you tell me about your childhood and how it all started – your awakening as an artist.

AI WEIWEI: Well, I was born in 1957. My father, Ai Qing, was a poet. As I was growing up he was criticized as a writer and punished and sent away to the Gobi desert in the northwest. So I basically spent sixteen years of my childhood and my youth in the Xinjiang Province, which is a remote area of China, near the Russian border. Living conditions were extremely harsh, and education was almost non-existent. But I grew up within the Cultural Revolution, and we had to exercise and study criticism, from self-criticism to political articles by Chairman Mao and Karl Marx, Lenin and such. That was an everyday exercise and formed the constant political surroundings. After Chairman Mao died I got into film university, at the Beijing Film Academy.

HUO: In this province the living conditions were harsh but I suppose because of your father, who was an extraordinary poet, you were also surrounded by his knowledge and literature. How was your relationship with him?

AWW: My father was a man who really loved art. He studied art in the 1930s in Paris. He was a very good artist. But right after he came back he was put in jail in Shanghai by the Kuomintang. So while in jail for three years he couldn't paint, of course, but he became a writer. He was heavily influenced by French poets – Apollinaire, Rimbaud, Baudelaire, you know, all this group of people – and he became a top figure in contemporary language poetry, but even then he couldn't write; it was forbidden in communist society. As a writer he was accused of being an anti-revolutionary, anti-Communist Party and anti-people, and that was a big crime. During the Cultural Revolution he was punished with hard labour and had to clean the public toilets for a village of about 200 people. It was quite a severe punishment for what he had done. He was almost sixty and he had never done any physical work. So for five years he never really had a chance to rest, even for one day. He often joked; he said, 'You know, people never stop shitting.' If he stopped one day, the next day's work would be exactly doubled and he wouldn't be able to handle it. He physically worked hard but he really handled this job well. I often used to go and visit him at those toilets, to watch what he was doing. I was too small to help. He would make this public area very clean – extremely, precisely clean – then go to another one. So that's my childhood education.

HUO: So no discussions with him about literature and art?

AWW: He would often talk about it. You know, we had to burn all his books because he could have got into trouble. We burned all those beautiful hardcover books he collected, and catalogues – beautiful museum catalogues. He only had one book left, which was a big French encyclopaedia. Every day he took notes from that book. He wrote Roman history. So he often taught us what the Romans did at the time – you know, who killed whom, all those stories – in the Gobi desert, which is so crazy. Soon he lost the vision in one of his eyes because of a lack of nutrition. But he talked about art, the Impressionists. He loved Rodin and Renoir, and he often talked about modern poetry.

HUO: Did your father resume his work later on?

AWW: In the 1980s he regained his honour. He was rehabilitated and very popular again. He became head of a writer's association. And he started to write like young people do, like a younger man. He was really passionate and a very nice man.

HUO: Is he still alive?

AWW: He passed away in 1996. His illness was what brought me back from the United States in 1993. He passed away when he was eighty-six.

HUO: You grew up in the province. Then when you were about twenty you moved to Beijing, where you enrolled in school.

AWW: That was right after Chairman Mao died. Nixon had been to China a few years earlier, and they realized they couldn't survive this communist struggle. You know, the United States were considered as an enemy, but that's more historical. What really endangered China was Russia, the big bear right above China. Russians and Chinese never trusted each other. So I think that's why, when Chairman Mao signalled the United States, Nixon and Kissinger had this so-called 'ping pong diplomacy'. After that, in 1976 a big earthquake in Tangshan killed 300,000 people in one night. And the same year, Mao died and three top leaders died – Zhou Enlai and another one. So China was becoming homeless, literally. The ideology collapsed, and the struggle failed and didn't know where to go. Politically it was an empty space. That's also the period when I had just graduated from high school. I spent some time in Beijing accompanying my father to treatment for his eye. I started to do some artworks, mostly because I wanted to escape the society. So I had a chance to learn some art from his friends.

HUO: Who were these people?

AWW: They were a group of literary men or artists who belonged to the same category as my father – they all became what's known as an 'enemy of the state' and then had nothing to do because all of the universities did not open. Many of them are still considered socially danger-ous and, like my father, politically still haven't had a chance to be rehabilitated. Basically they're professors and very knowledgeable men and literary men or artists, good art-ists. They had a huge influence on me.

HUO: How was it at that time, in the late 1970s, with regard to Western art? What were its influences? Were there books or illustrations?

AWW: There were almost no books. The whole nation was to have no single book. I got my first book on Van

Gogh, Degas and Manet and another one, Jasper Johns, from a translator. His name was Jian Sheng Yee. He married, I think, a woman from Germany, and so he had a chance to get those books, and he gave them to me. He thought, 'Ah this kid loves art.' And those books became so valuable. You know, everyone shared them in Beijing – this very little circle of artists, everybody read those few copies. It's very interesting that we all liked the post-Impressionists but we threw the Jasper Johns away because we couldn't understand it. We asked 'What is this?', and the American flag or a map.

HUO: It went into the garbage?

AWW: Straight to the garbage. From the education we received at that time we had no clue as to what this was. There was no university education in the Cultural Revolution. They followed the socialist rules, in the Russian style.

HUO: There was no knowledge of Marcel Duchamp or Barnett Newman?

AWW: No, absolutely nothing. The knowledge stopped at Cubism. Picasso and Matisse were the last heroes of modern history.

HUO: This is fascinating: there was a limited range of knowledge and hardly any information or books, and yet between the late 1970s and the 1980s there was a dynamic avant-garde in China, of which you were a protagonist. What happened during that period? There was no information, there was still a lot of oppression and difficulty, and yet in this resistance somehow an incredible generation formed and became to China what the 1960s generation was to Europe and America, when the Western world experienced this incredible expansion of art at the time – Andy Warhol, Joseph Beuys.

AWW: I'm very glad you pointed this out. We are a generation that had a sense of the past, which is the time of the Iron Curtain and of the communist struggle. It was a tough political struggle – it was against humanism and individualism and there was, as you know, strong censorship of anything not coming from China. It was even more severe than in North Korea today. The only poetry you could recite was about Chairman Mao. Every classroom, every paper we read was about Chairman Mao, his language and his image. But we all knew what happened before that in the 1920s and 1930s. We all knew about our parents' fights for a new China, a modern China with a democracy and a science. And then suddenly they had a chance, in the late 1970s and early 1980s, to rethink that part of history. We started to realize that the lack of freedom and freedom of expression is what caused China's tragedy. So this group of young people started to write poetry and to make magazines, adopting a democratic way of thinking. We started to act really self-consciously and with a self-awareness to try to achieve this – to fight for personal freedom.

It was like spring had come. Everybody would read whatever book they had. There were no copy machines, so we would copy the whole book by hand and give it to a friend. There was a really limited amount of 'nutrition' and information, but it was passed on with such effort and such a passionate love for art and rational political thinking. That was the first genuine moment of our democracy.

HUO: I always felt that it was like a new avant-garde movement. How did people meet? Was there a bar or a school?

AWW: There was a wall. We called it 'the Democratic Wall'. People could post their writings or thoughts on the wall. We used to meet there. And there was a very small circle – China has a huge population, but there were only maybe less than a hundred people who were so active. There were about twenty or thirty magazines we were writing every night, and we had to print them and post them on the wall.

HUO: Did you make these magazines yourself?

AWW: I did some. I drew a cover by hand for a poet who, at that time, was the best poet. Every cover I drew by hand. So we published books, but then in 1980 Deng Xiaoping came up and repressed the movement. He denounced the wall. He was so afraid of social change – they wanted to have some change, but they didn't want anybody to denounce the communist struggle.

HUO: Did you start to make artworks at the time? What is your very earliest artwork?

AWW: I started as a painter. I made drawings, a lot of drawings. I would spend months in the train station because there were so many people there, they were like free models for me – of course at that time there was no model and no school. So I would just stay in the train station to draw all those people who were waiting there.

HUO: Do you still have these drawings?

AWW: I think my mother threw away most of them. You know, being an artist was not a prestigious practice at that time. I also spent time in the zoo, making very nice drawings of the animals. That was my starting point.

HUO: What were your earliest paintings like?

AWW: They were mostly about landscapes, in the fashion of Munch – or some were even in the fashion of Cézanne. You can clearly see it. I remember, at the end of the school, the teacher would give a critique to every student but he purposely left me alone.

HUO: You were in your own world.

AWW: Yes, I was very clearly already on my own. I left school before I got to graduate – to go to the United States, in 1981.

HUO: What prompted you to go to the United States?

AWW: In my mind I already thought New York was the capital of contemporary art. And I wanted to be on top. On the way to the airport my mum said things like 'Do you feel sad because you don't speak English?', 'You have no money' (I had thirty dollars in my hand) and

'What are you going to do there?' I said, 'I am going home.' My mother was so surprised, and so were my classmates. I said, 'Maybe ten years later, when I come back, you'll see another Picasso!' They all laughed. I was so naïve, but I had so much confidence. I left because the activists from our same group were put in jail. The accusation was that they were spies for the West, which was total nonsense. The leaders of the Democratic Movement were put in jail for thirteen years, and we knew all these people, and we all got absolutely mad and even scared – you know, 'this nation has no hope.'

HUO: And so you arrived in the United States. At the time there were very different tendencies – a neo-expressionist, neo-figurative wave and at the same time Neo-Geo and appropriation art. How did you fit into this New York art world?

AWW: At the very beginning I studied English. I was so sure I would spend my whole life in New York, I told people this was the last place I would be for the rest of my time (even though I was just in my twenties). When my English was okay, I enrolled in the Parsons School of Design. My teacher was Sean Scully. He liked Jasper Johns, who had just had a show with a series of new works at Leo Castelli at the time. The first book I read was *The Philosophy of Andy Warhol: (From A to B and Back Again)*. I loved that book. The language is so simple and beautiful. So from that I started to know all. I became a fan of Johns, and then I got introduced to Duchamp's thinking, which was my introduction to modern and contemporary histories like Dada and Surrealism. I was so fascinated with that period and of course what was going on in New York. It was, as you said, the early 1980s neo-expressionism, which I practised a little bit but really didn't like. My mind is more about ideas, so I really liked Conceptualism and Fluxus. But of course at that time it wasn't popular at home. The 1980s were so much about neo-expressionism. You had to attend those galleries and also the East Village. And there was such a big mix and also a struggle. You started asking yourself what kind of artist you wanted to be. Then Jeff Koons and the others came out with such a fresh approach. I still remember Koons' first show with all those basketballs in the fish tanks. It was just next door in my neighbourhood, the East Village. And I liked that work so much, and the price was very low, 3,000 dollars or something. I was so fascinated by that.

HUO: When did you start working with sculpture and installation?

AWW: I did my first sculpture in 1983, if you could call it sculpture. Later I used something like a coat hanger to make Duchamp's profile (*Hanging Man*, 1985). That time I had already done violins (*Violin*, 1985), and I had attached condoms to an army raincoat (*Safe Sex*, 1986). It was about safe sex because around that time everybody was so scared about AIDS. People had just recognized the disease and had more fear than knowledge about it. I really wanted to work with everyday objects – it was the influence of Dada and Duchamp – but I didn't do much. There are only a few objects left because every time I moved – and I moved about ten times in ten years in New York – I had to throw away all the works.

HUO: The violin is interesting because it's very much related to Surrealism. Does it still exist?

AWW: Yes, that's true. It's so funny – it's a commentary about an old time under the present conditions.

HUO: You were still painting at that time. There are the three portraits of Mao: *Mao 1-3* (1985). When did you decide to stop painting?

AWW: Those were the last paintings I did. I did those Maos, and it was somehow like saying goodbye to the old times. I did the group over a very short period, and then I just gave up painting altogether.

HUO: How about drawing? I saw a lot of drawings in your studio. Is drawing still a daily practice?

AWW: The early drawings I made were more for training myself in how to handle the world with the very simple traces of a mark. That can be enjoyable. I did the best drawings, so even my teachers at the time loved them. They'd say, 'This guy can draw so well,' but there is always the danger of becoming self-indulgent. If you see drawings made by Picasso and Matisse, you see they keep drawing because they can just do it so well. I don't like that kind of feeling, so whenever I begin to feel okay then I try to refuse it and escape from it. Later on I made drawings with different methods. I take photos every day, which, to me, is just like drawing. It's an exercise about what you see and how you record it. And to try to not use your hands but rather to use your vision and your mind.

HUO: I see you always have your little digital camera with you. You photograph a lot and that's also a form of drawing, almost like a sketchbook. We could call them 'mind drawings'. When did you start taking photographs?

AWW: I started in the late 1980s in New York, when I gave up painting. There were only fifty top artists at that time, with Julian Schnabel and those people. I had to attend all those openings and those galleries, and I knew that there was no chance for me. So I started to take a lot of photos, thousands of photos, mostly in black and white. I didn't even develop them. They were all there until I went back to Beijing. I developed them ten years later. Taking photos is like breathing. It becomes part of you.

HUO: That's like a blog before the blog.

AWW: Much later, about two or three years ago, they set up this blog for me – I didn't even know what to do. I realized I could put my photos on it, so I put up almost 70,000 photos, at least a hundred photos a day, so that they could be shared by thousands of people. The blog has already been visited by over 4 million people. It's such a wonderful thing, the Internet. People who don't know me can see exactly what I've been doing.

HUO: So now it's basically just a continuum of hundreds of thousands of images, and it's an ever-growing archive. But do you continue to draw? I'm very interested in the link to calligraphy, this fluid calligraphy, and the kinds of geometry and fragments and the layering and composing of space.

Zaha Hadid once told me that there's really a link between calligraphy and current computer drawing.

AWW: Calligraphy is the traces of a mind, or maybe an emotion or thought. Now, with a computer you have photo images, you have the radio. Calligraphy is no longer the matter of hand. I do interviews, hundreds of interviews a year. There are all kinds of sources: newspapers, magazines, television, on all matters — art, design, architecture, social political commentary and criticism. I think we have a chance today to become everything and nothing at the same time. We can become part of a reality but we can be totally lost and not know what to do.

HUO: You mentioned criticism. In your early days writing was very important. You've had this link to poetry, and you're still writing a lot.

AWW: I like writing the most. If I have to value it against all human activities, writing is the most interesting form, because it relates to everybody and it's a form that everybody can understand. During the Cultural Revolution we never had a chance to write, besides writing some critical stuff, so I really like to pick up on that, and the blog gives me a chance. I did a lot of interviews with artists, just simple interviews. I asked about their past, what's on their minds, and I also wrote. So in the blog I did over 200 pieces of writing and interviews which really put me in a critical position — you have to write it down, it's black and white, it's in words, and they can see it, so you really have no place to escape. I really love it, and I think it's important for you, as a person, to exercise, to clear out what you really want to say. Maybe you're just empty, but maybe you really have to define this emptiness and to be clear.

HUO: Your blog and your work make a lot of things public. Do you have any secrets? What is your best-kept secret?

AWW: I have a tendency to open up the personal secrets. I think, being human, that both life and death have a secret side but there's the temptation to reveal the truth and to see the fact that you need some courage or understanding about life or death. So, even if you try to reveal or open yourself, you're still a mystery, because everybody is a mystery. We can never understand ourselves. However we act or whatever we do is misleading. So in that case, it doesn't matter.

HUO: Now, we're still in New York, we are in the 1980s, and at a certain moment you decided to go back to China. Was that a planned decision or did it have to do with, as you said, your father getting ill? I spoke to I. M. Pei, who said that when he left for the United States it was a departure without return. He became an American architect and didn't go back. So what about this idea of exile – temporary exile or permanent exile?

AWW: I stayed in New York. I gave up my legal status because I knew I was going to stay there forever, so I become an illegal alien. I tried to survive by doing any kind of work that came to hand – I did gardening at the beginning, and housekeeping. At that time my English was quite bad. Then I did carpentry, I did framing work, I had a printing job, I did all sorts of work just to survive, but at the same time I knew I was an artist. It became like a symbolic thing to be 'an artist'. You're not just somebody else, but an artist. But I wasn't making so much art. After Duchamp, I realized that being an artist is more about a lifestyle and attitude than producing some product.

HUO: More like an attitude?

AWW: More like an attitude, a way of looking at things. So that freed me, but at the same time it put me in a very difficult position – I knew I was an artist but didn't do so much. So the few works we see today are probably the only works I did. I was just wandering around. I didn't have much to do. And after a while it became very difficult, because I was so young. On the one hand you want to do something, to be somebody, but at the same time you realize it's almost impossible, economically and culturally. It was an excuse for me to go back to China and to take a look, because for the past twelve years I hadn't written back home and had never visited. I didn't have a good relationship with my family. There was some distance. The question was, if I had to go back, this was the moment. So in 1993 I made a decision and just packed everything and moved back.

HUO: How did you find China changed?

AWW: 1989 was the crackdown of the student movement: Tiananmen. I had no illusions about China, even though everybody told me that China had changed so much and that I should take a look. Some things had changed, some things hadn't changed. What changed was that there was more beauty in the centre. It was a little bit looser about the economy. There was little bit of free enterprise, but there was still a strong struggle, the ideology. And what hasn't changed is the Communist Party – it's still wide, still kills today. There's still censorship, there's no freedom of speech, just the same as when I left. It's crazy. It's really such a complex set of conditions. And you realize the society has so many problems and the change is so small and so insignificant and so slow. After I got back, I still felt there wasn't much to do there, so I started working on three books.

HUO: That's the beginning of your famous books.

AWW: Yes. *The Black Book* (1994) is the first one, then the *White* (1995) and the *Grey* (1997).

HUO: I saw them in an exhibition at the Victoria and Albert Museum in London about design in China. They're cult books now.

AWW: There are so many artists who have been influenced by those three books, and so I tried to make a document or an archive for what was going on, and at the same time to promote a conceptual base for the art rather than just art on canvas on easels. So I forced artists to write a concept, to explain what is behind their activity. At the very beginning they were not used to it, but some knew how to do it. I also wanted to introduce Duchamp, Jeff Koons and Andy Warhol and some conceptual artists, and the essential writings, to China.

HUO: Was this the beginning of your curatorial endeavour? You could say these books are also curatorial projects and that you've curated ever since.

AWW: Yes, it's curatorial. So around 1997/98 we created this China Art Archives and Warehouse, the first alternative space for contemporary art in China. Before that all the works were sold in hotel lobbies, and framing shops were just for the tourists and foreign embassies. So we did it and tried to justify the space and the institution to show what was happening. And then later, by 2000, I curated another show, 'Fuck Off,' in Shanghai. I think we met before that.

HUO: Yeah, we met for the first time in the late 1990s.

AWW: At that time you were so young and so fresh, and I still remember the evening we were in an artist's home, I think – many people gathered to see you.

HUO: I remember. That first trip to China was essential to me. I'd like to stay a little bit more with the *Black*, *White* and *Grey* books. Looking at these books today they appear like avant-garde manifestos, to some extent. We live in a time where there are fewer manifestos. Dadaism and Futurism, for example, both had manifestos in the early twentieth century, but still in the 1960s there was this whole new avant-garde idea – Benjamin Buchloh always spoke about the whole idea of the manifesto. Do you think there is still space for this kind of movement?

AWW: I think art always has a manifesto, any good art,

as with the Dada movement or early Russian Constructivism or early Fluxus in the 1970s, all those things that people did. It's an announcement of the new, an announcement to be part of a new position or a justification, or to identify the possible conditions. I think that's the most exciting part about art. Once you make a manifesto you really take some risks. You have to put yourself in a condition. You have to be singled out because it's the nature of the manifesto.

HUO: In architecture, manifestos are a very different thing. You started, at a certain moment, to venture into architecture. Did it begin in America or did it start when you went back to China? When I met you in the 1990s you were already in a double practice – as both artist and architect.

AWW: I didn't start consciously. I remember two instances I had with architecture. First was discovering Frank Lloyd Wright, only because he did the Guggenheim, and that beauty we hated because ... you know, no painting could be hung there. (That was then, but now I think it's very interesting. It's just like a parking lot type of thing). The second was when I bought a book by Wittgenstein, the writer-philosopher. He did this building for his sister in Vienna. I saw that book and thought, 'Oh, this guy can build a house for his sister,' so I bought that beautiful book. Those are the only two instances in New York that I had a relationship with architecture. After I came back I lived with my mother in Beijing. In 1999 I decided to have my own studio. So I walked into this village and asked the owner of the village if I could rent some land. He said, 'Yes we have land,' so I said, 'Can I build something?' He said,

'Yes, you can build.' It was illegal, but they didn't care. So I rented the land, and one afternoon I made some drawings, without even thinking about architecture. I just used pure measurement for the volume and proportions and put in a window, a door. Then six days later we had already finished it, and then I moved in. This was the time when China started to build a lot, but many of the buildings were very commercial and came from just one single kind of practice. So a lot of magazines noticed: 'Oh, we can build differently, here's this guy who builds with very limited resources, for a very low price, by himself.' It became a very widely exposed building in China. People started asking me to do work for them, some big commercial projects. So I decided, 'This is so simple. You just use your common knowledge and you don't have to be an architect to build,' because I think that the so-called 'common knowledge' and everyday experience are so lacking in academic studies. I had a chance, and I had nothing else to do, so I started a practice. I formed this company, FAKE Design. In China the word 'fake' is pronounced 'fuck'. We have done about fifty projects in the past seven years. All kinds of projects, from urban planning to interior design.

HUO: Most of them are built, right?

AWW: Ninety per cent of them are built.

HUO: You have built more in nine years as an artist than many architects in a lifetime.

AWW: Yes, it's true, we build more than most architects in their lifetime.

HUO: What an achievement. Not only have you built a lot, but you have also curated the most visionary architecture projects. When we spoke last time for *Domus* you were curating an architecture village, almost like Weissenhofsiedlung from the 1920s in Stuttgart, in which modern architects build a street. Now you're working on an even bigger architecture project involving one hundred architects. Could you talk a little bit about this? Curating architecture is very different from curating art. Curating architecture is production of reality.

AWW: Yes, I love the words 'production of reality'. Architecture is important for a time because it's a physical example of who we are, of how we look at ourselves, of how we want to identify with our time, so it's evidence of mankind at the time. After the first venture into architecture, I fell very much in love with this activity. It relates so directly to politics and reality. Then I realized that it's very important for China and for the world to be introduced to each other. So many young architects are produced in the West but have no chance to build their work, and their knowledge can never be exercised. Education itself has failed because you only just theoretically talk about architecture, and this becomes another kind of architecture. I thought it would be best to have them take part in global activities, the reality. Also in another way it is important to balance the view of architecture. It's not just education through the examples of so-called masterpieces. It's also the study of real locations, real problems, and needs to include the undesirable conditions like high speed or vast developments or low-cost architecture.

I think those are important factors of architecture but aren't always being consciously brought out.

HUO: Low-cost architecture – that's like low-cost airlines.

AWW: Yes, or rough architecture, which is fine. It's all about human struggle and the reality of the condition rather than being a utopian thing. That's why I try to curate the architecture projects, to try and bring as many young people from all over the world as possible, because they all want to exercise their own mind and their own problems. The problems are their own problem. Any problem is everybody's problem, so you just have to participate. And if you have no chance to participate, this is a pity!

HUO: So that leads to your biggest project, the one with one hundred architects in Inner Mongolia.

AWW: Yes. A developer asked me to help build this town in Inner Mongolia. They said, 'We think you're the one that can make things happen.' I said yes. I thought about it because I had announced that I would totally give up architecture because I had so much work to do. But I thought, 'Okay, I can do it, but only if I'm in the position of curating it, because I don't care if I actually build one myself. I don't have that ego anymore, but I know many great minds, young minds, who would love to do something and this is the chance.' So he understood me. He said, 'Whatever you say is fine.' So I asked Jacques

[Herzog] and I said, 'Jacques, you know this is a big project, but your participation is to give me the list of names.' And Jacques understood immediately. I don't think it required much explanation. Soon after, he provided a list of names. So we contacted those one hundred people, and they all agreed to come. The first sixty are already there, and a group of thirty are going next month. There will be a total of one hundred architects who, maybe with their partners, will make two or three hundred people gathering in this Mongolian town, in the middle of the desert. They're going to start to build there. It will be ready in two years' time.

HUO: What a miracle!

AWW: I think finally we realized this kind of miracle can happen in a short period of time, and I do have an impact, not only for those architects who are participating but also for the people of the world to see the possibilities. I think that's what's good about it.

HUO: This is a very special moment in your work because we started out with China and then New York and now, fifteen years later, after leaving New York, you're back to New York with a big exhibition, which just opened last week at Mary Boone. It goes full circle – as a young artist you went to see exhibitions at Mary Boone, and now you're exhibiting there too.

AWW: It's so funny. It's such an unbelievable circumstance. In the 1980s I used to go to Mary Boone to see what was going on, and one day, years later, I was walking in

Beijing and got a phone call from Mary, and she said she would like to have a show with me. I was so happy I immediately accepted. It's so strange the whole feeling. In New York you think you can never ever do it, and then many years later it becomes possible. Karen Smith curated the show, and it turned out to be a big, well-received show, and so many people went to see it and talked a lot about it. Mary was so very happy about the collaboration. She asked me to do a chandelier, and I hesitated because I have done several before. But I like to work within demands or requirements, so I made a chandelier that is falling down from the ceiling and landing on the ground (*Descending Light*, 2007). We did the whole thing so quickly, I didn't even have time to really assemble it completely. We just had to send all the parts to New York, and over twenty people assembled it in the gallery. Now it looks fantastic there.

HUO: So it's really the idea of light falling. It's a descendence.

AWW: Yes, it's really about that.

HUO: It's also a follow-up from a great piece I saw in Liverpool, *Fountain of Light* (2007), which was about the Russian avant-garde.

AWW: I think the early Russian avant-garde had a great mind. They had such imagination and innovation about what the coming century was going to be about. Of course there was a lot of utopian thinking, and many things stayed utopian rather than becoming a reality. So when I was offered this project in Liverpool I immediately thought about Vladimir Tatlin's *Monument to the Third International*. It would come as a commentary or a pun about the beginning of the industrial age, during which England was an important factor, and the beginning of the information age and globalization. So I decided to make this light fountain floating in the water.

HUO: It's also so interesting because you made it at the beginning of the twenty-first century, and when Tatlin did it it had to do with the future and with the twentieth century. Now we're in 2008, already eight years into the first decade, which is nearly over. It doesn't really have a name yet – 'zero zero'? It's a very strange moment. So how do you see the future? Are you optimistic?

AWW: When we talk about the future we become so naïve – whatever we say is not going to be happen, so whatever happens is beyond whatever we can imagine. It's just so crazy.

HUO: When I was looking at your book *Works 2004-2007* last night I became aware once more of all the different production practices present in your work. We've spoken about architecture, we've spoken about curating, and we've spoken about your sculpture and installations. There are so many fascinating aspects that have started to unfold over the last couple of years. I remember two years ago I saw *Bowl of Pearls* (2006) for the first time in your studio. We are living in the digital age, when we're accumulating more and more archive material but not necessarily memory. A lot of your works are about memory: and there is *Coca-Cola Vase* (1997) but then at the same time there is also the work with furniture, like *Table with Two Legs on the Wall* (1997), which revisits memory in an interesting way. Could we talk about memory? Eric Hobsbawm was saying to me the other day that we should protest against forgetting.

AWW: Yes, because we move so fast that a memory is something we can grab. It's the easiest thing to just attach to during fast movement. The faster we move, the more often we turn our heads back to look on the past, and this is all because we move so fast. The work in the catalogue may be just one-tenth of my activities. On the one hand I take art very seriously, but the production has never been so serious, and most of it it's an ironic act. But, anyhow, you need traces, you need people to be able to locate you, you have a responsibility to say what you have to say and to be wherever you should be. You're part of the misery and you can't make it more or less. You're still part of the whole fascinating condition here. I work now in a different sense, but it's really just traces. It's not important. It's not the work itself. It's a fragment that shows there was a storm passing by. Those pieces are left because they're evidence, but they really cannot construct something. It's a waste.

HUO: A waste? Because you call them fragments, these are fragments, no?

AWW: It's weird, because you call something something else. For example, an old, destroyed temple: you know the old temple was beautiful and beautifully built. We could once all believe and hope in it. But once it has been destroyed, it's nothing. It becomes another artist's material to build something completely contradictory to what it was before. So it's full of ignorance and also a redefinition or reconsideration. All those Neolithic vases are from 4,000 years ago and have been dipped into a Japanese-brand industrial household paint, and they become another image entirely, with the original image hiding in thin layers (or thick layers) of this paint. People can still recognize them, and for that reason they value them, because they move from the traditional antique museum into a contemporary art environment, and they appear in auctions or as some kind of collector's item.

HUO: Besides the fragments and the waste, a sort of monumental junkyard piece here plays a role. At *Documenta*, seeing your *Fairytale* (2007) and looking at your blog, increasingly I came to think that your blog is actually a social sculpture in a Joseph Beuys kind of sense. Do you see yourself as a social sculptor, and is there a link to Beuys?

AWW: I think you're the first one who has recognized that in the digital age virtual reality is part of reality, and it becomes more and more influential in our daily lives. Think about how many people use or are addicted to it. And of course all activities or artworks should be social. Even in the medieval age they all carried this message of a social and politically strong mind. From the Renaissance to the best of contemporary art, it's about, as you said, the manifestos and our individuality. Especially today I think it's unavoidable to be social and political. So in that sense I think Beuys made a very good example to initiate his pupils. I know very little about Beuys because I studied in the United States, but Warhol did it in his own ways: his factory, his announcements about 'popism', about portraits, about production, the interviews he did – nothing could be more social than that, I think.

HUO: Now we've spoken a lot about your manifold projects, but what we haven't spoken about is my favourite question, your yet-unrealized projects. I think I've asked you before, but I think I'll have to ask you today again. What are your yet-unrealized projects?

AWW: I think it would be to disappear. Nothing could be bigger than that. After a while everybody just wants to disappear. Otherwise, I don't know. So far, practically speaking, I will have a show in Haus der Kunst in Munich next year, so I have to prepare for that and several other shows. I don't know. I don't know what's going to come out, how it's going to be handled.

HUO: Dan Graham once said that the only way to fully understand artists is to know what music they listen to. What kind of music are you listening to?

AWW: I don't listen to music at home. I have never in my life turned on music. I'm not conscious of music. I can appreciate it, I can analyse it, and I have many friends in music, but I never really turn on to music. Silence is my music.

HUO: What is your favourite word?

AWW: My favourite word? It's 'act'.

HUO: What turns you on?

AWW: The unfamiliar reality. The condition of uneasiness.

HUO: What turns you off?

AWW: Repetition.

HUO: What's the moment we are all waiting for?

AWW: The moment where we lose our consciousness.

HUO: What profession other than yours would you like to attempt?

AWW: To live without thinking about professions.

HUO: Hypothetically, if heaven exists, what would you like to hear God say when you arrive?

AWW: 'Oh! You're not supposed to be here.'

This interview was conducted for the definitive monograph Ai Weiwei *(Phaidon Press, 2009), which also features essays by Karen Smith, Bernard Fibicher and Ai Weiwei and includes over 160 images.*

Mapping

In 2010 we ran the Serpentine Map Marathon in London at the Royal Geographic Society. We invited Ai Weiwei to be part of it. Mapping is a very exciting field, one of the major topics on the Internet, what with Google Earth and new navigation systems. Maps – and this is true also for Ai Weiwei's work in general – produce new realities as much as they seek to document current ones. Maps go beyond the spacetime of the present. This interview addresses navigational and cartographic strategies in Ai Weiwei's work. In the week that it was recorded Ai Weiwei also inaugurated his installation in the Tate Turbine Hall.

HUO: Today we are going to talk about your maps. There are many different maps. I don't know where we should start; shall we start with the images you are showing? I spoke to Uli Sigg the other day, who was here in London. Uli was telling me that he had had a conversation once with you about fractals and about Benoit Mandelbrot. I would be very curious to know what was important for you about the fractals of Mandelbrot, which somehow triggered your first maps.

AWW: Well, he tried to explain this theory of fractals to me. I tried to understand it, but I figured out it's not possible for me to really understand it. So I made this map of China. The map is about territory; it's about boundary and relations to different kinds of political conditions. I made the map and later I showed it to the Chinese Embassy; and they sent some political bureau to check if I really showed a piece of land that was there, because then the Ambassador could come and see it, so it has to be really correct. So Taiwan is there, Hong Kong is there. But it is a map I present, and if Taiwan is present on a map then Outer Mongolia also would be there. China has really been changing all the time, and it's very hard to see what is the correct one, and it is dependent on really different political conditions. But after you make one it is always solid, people think it's real, so I decided to make that one then forget about the theory as it's very complicated.

HUO: There are actually several of them. We have an image here. Can you tell us about these maps of China?

AWW: I did those maps actually with an old temple that was turned down for current development. So the Bordon temple was contracted now. It's a very traditional craft shape and the shape of the kind of joints on it become like a region or territory, like leaving marks on it. People often ask me if there are real political conditions represented here, but it's really according to the material and the possibility of how to make it.

HUO: Now, you very often return to China, to its history and people, particularly with this map, so China remains a central subject; and I was wondering why this is the case, why maps of China?

AWW: It's not so really intellectual: in it there are really a lot of pieces that are old, and I've constructed them together and . . .

HUO: There are many other maps. There are your digital maps, your video maps, and in the same book★ there is actually a very extraordinary map, which is really like a mind map, so maybe we could talk about this.

★ *Ways Beyond Art: Ai Weiwei* (2009), eds. Elena Ochoa Foster and Hans Ulrich Obrist.

AWW: Yes, that's a concept in which we really started to try to produce something about China; we tried to say how it related to the past and to the current situation and all the issues. But it always has to deal with time, and if you want to do something three-dimensional it's very difficult, it always has to be very flat and two-dimensional, and so it is through the Internet that it becomes possible to overcome the problem of describing time and place. But this is closer to reality, because in reality the time and the place are not really fixed, only the moment is fixed. So I spend a lot of time on Twitter and blogging. On Twitter I think you see a lot of dots – every tree, every person is a lot of dots on the map. It happens at random, you don't know who is sending it, and you can also answer them at very different times . . . actually it destroys the two-dimensional thinking of the map.

HUO: How did that start? Because I remember that when we met for the first time you had just started the blog. It was at the moment when Julia Peyton-Jones, Gunnar Kvaran and I were working on the China power station exhibition* and we included, translated for the first time into English, your blog, and in the meanwhile your blog has become such a public blog, and you have also used Twitter, hundreds of times a day sometimes . . . But how did all this start, how did you come into contact . . . ?

---

* CHINA POWER STATION: *Part 1*, exhibition at Battersea Power Station 8 October to 5 November 2006. A Serpentine exhibition in collaboration with the Astrup Fearnley Museum in Oslo, where CHINA POWER STATION: *Part 2* took place.

AWW: It all comes from difficulties, because you do not have normal Internet access in China due to this great firewall. The Great Wall is also about the mapping of the time, because it defines the land and defends China from the other nations. The great firewall is a design to block information, mainly from the West, I think. So it is a strong technical censor result, while in China of course you can access Twitter, or YouTube or Facebook or even Google. So you see how to maintain that kind of territory: not to be allowed freely across it is always the strong concern of a totalitarian society.

HUO: Very early on you used the blog not only for text: you have used them for so many images, particularly the blog. Can you tell us about this incredible use of so many, many images?

AWW: Only through the technique of a new science … you can create almost infinite power in one point, one dot. I can put up one solar image in a day or I can put up a couple of movies or endless conversations with just one touch of the keyboard, so that is what is really fascinating.

HUO: I know that you have got a plane to catch, but I have two more questions I wanted to ask you. There are many aspects of mapping in your practice, and I think there is one that should not be left untouched, and that is the one in your videos, because the work, for example for regional landscape, in your videos documents the ring roads in Beijing. Uli Sigg told me that he has always seen your videos and your photography of the ring roads as your mapping of Beijing, so I was wondering if you could tell us a little bit about how you map the city of Beijing through these works.

AWW: In 2003 I agreed to teach in Tsinghua Art University in China. You know I hate school, so I told the University that and said I can teach but we have to do the teaching in a bus, so we rented a big bus. We divided the Beijing map into sixteen parts, and each day the bus would go through all the streets, so one day the bus went through one part, the next day through the next part, but after sixteen – about 150 hours – we had really been through all the streets in Beijing. We had a video camera mounted in front of the bus to take the whole long video, lasting about six days and nights, and it tells the story of what Beijing would look like in this line. Of course, before and after we made the video, the city was always changing; we couldn't even find the same road again, it was being destroyed or rebuilt.

HUO: That makes it very difficult, I suppose, to map a city like Beijing, because European cities change so much more slowly than Chinese cities. Beijing has incredibly rapid change, so are you doing videos again and again, is this an ongoing work, or is that form of mapping concluded?

AWW: I did three or four videos of the same nature; I made one line across Beijing, which is 43 kilometres. Every 50 metres would take one minute's video, so in all over 10 hours video is needed to see this line, this axis through the city. So we made a second video, a third video, to define the differences, you know, the second video to show rainy days, the third to show sunny days . . . it's really an effort, which doesn't mean anything actually: it's about trying to make an effort which is going to be different the next day.

HUO: To see all these themes would be a marathon in itself, I suppose. My very last question, as we look here at these extraordinary videos – I wonder if you could tell us a little bit more about your idea of the sunflower seeds and how this piece came about – what was the epiphany of this piece?

AWW: Well, about this piece, I have really talked to so many journalists that I don't think I really have much to say about it. It is a piece that is really for people to look at.

HUO: Wonderful, thank you so much Ai Weiwei.

Acknowledgements

With particular thanks to Uli Sigg and Phil Tinari.

Grateful acknowledgement is made for permission to reprint the following material:

Part II of 'Digital Architecture : Analogue Architecture' was first published in *Domus*, 894 (July–August 2006), courtesy Editoriale Domus S.p.A., Rozzano, Milano, Italy, all rights reserved. Parts I and II were published in Hans Ulrich Obrist, *The China Interviews*, ed. Phil Tinari and Angie Baecker, Office for Discourse Engineering (2009). A different version of this interview was published in Hans Ulrich Obrist, *Interviews Volume 2*, ed. Charles Arsène-Henry, Shumon Basar and Karen Marta, Charta (2010).

'The Many Dimensions of Ai Weiwei' was first published in *Ways Beyond Art*, ed. Elena Ochoa Foster and Hans Ulrich Obrist, Ivory Press (2009).

'The Retrospective' was first published in Karen Smith, Hans Ulrich Obrist and Bernard Fibicher, *Ai Weiwei*, Phaidon Press (2009).

The 'Sustainability' interview first appeared in *A Post-Olympic Beijing Mini-Marathon*, Vitamin Creative Space and JRP|Ringier (2010).

With thanks to: Charles Arsène-Henry, Angie Baecker, Katy Banyard, Shumon Basar, Imogen Boase, Stefano Boeri, Erica Bolton, Laura Bossi, John Brockman, Hubert Burda, Patrick Bussman, Helen Conford, Kevin Conroy

Scott, Melanie Cousins, Steffi Czerny, David Davies, Rose Dempsey, Chris Dercon, Iñaki Domingo, Richard Duguid, Olafur Eliasson, FAKE Archive, Hu Fang, Carmen Figini, Elena Ochoa Foster, Norman Foster, Craig Garrett, Joseph Grima, Hou Hanru, Jacques Herzog, Koo Jeong-A, Bettina Korek, Gunnar Kvaran, Nicola Lees, Giuseppe Liverani, Nicolas Logsdail, Karen Marta, Stefan McGrath, Urs Meile, Pierre de Meuron, Ella Obrist, Julia Peyton-Jones, Lucia Pietroiusti, Marcel Reichart, Michele Robecchi, Richard Schlagman, Urs Stahel, Sally Tallant, Phil Tinari, Lorraine Two, Zhang Wei, Shaway Yeh.